"Anyone Who Has Taken Birth As A Human Being
In India Bharata-Bhumi"
Shambhu Dasa

"Anyone Who Has Taken Birth As A Human Being In India Bharata-Bhumi"

Shambhu Dasa

Contents

Preface   13

Introduction   15

Acknowledgments   19

1. SRI ISOPANISHAD   21
Text 3

2. SRIMAD-BHAGAVATAM   27
Canto 4 Chapter 23 Text 28

3. CONVERSATION DR. BENFORD   31

4. SRIMAD-BHAGAVATAM   35
Canto 7 Chapter 6 Text 1

5. SRIMAD BHAGAVATAM   41
Canto 7 Chapter 6 Text 2

6. SRIMAD BHAGAVATAM   45
Canto 7 Chapter 6 Text 14

7. SRIMAD BHAGAVATAM   47
Canto 7 Chapter 6 Text 15

8. SECTARIANISM   49

9. SANATANA DHARMA   53

10. SRIMAD BHAGAVATAM   65
Canto 5 Chapter 19 Text 21

11. SRIMAD BHAGAVATAM   69
Canto 5 Chapter 19 Text 22

12. SRIMAD BHAGAVATAM   73
Canto 5 Chapter 19 Text 23

13. SRIMAD BHAGAVATAM   77
Canto 5 Chapter 19 Text 25

14. SRIMAD BHAGAVATAM   81
Canto 5 Chapter 19 Text 28

15. SRIMAD BHAGAVATAM   85
Canto 5 Chapter 19 Text 19

16. SRIMAD BHAGAVATAM   89
Canto 6 Chapter 16 Text 58

17. SRIMAD BHAGAVATAM   91
Canto 5 Chapter 19 Text 24

18. SRI CHAITANYA CHARITAMRTA   95
(Madhya-lila 25.26)

19. ROOM CONVERSATION, MORNING WALKS ETC.   107
- Conversation with LT. David Mozee Chicago Police dept. July 1975   107
- Room Conversation: June 29, 1972   109
- University Lecture Calcutta, January 29, 1973   111
- Room Conversation with Sanskrit Professor 8/13/1973-Paris   122
- Room Conversations, Vrndavana India, 9/11/1974   122
- Room Conversation, Atlanta GA, 3/2/1975   123
- Morning Walk 3/11/1975, London   124
- Room Conversation with Indian Guest 3/13/1975, Tehran   125
- Morning Walk 6/13/1976, Detroit   126
- Interview with Prof. O'Connel, Motilal and Shivaram 6/18/1976 Toronto   126
- Room Conversation 6/24/1976 New Vrndavana   127
- Evening Darshana 7/11/1976, New York   128
- Room Conversation 8/2/1976 New Mayapur (French-Farm)   129
- Evening Darshan 8/10/1976, Tehran   130
- Room Conversation 8/14/1976, Mumbai   130
- Morning Walk 8/23/1976, Hyderabad   132

- Room Conversation with Mr. Tombe
(M.L.A.) 12/25/1976, Mumbai   133
- Morning Walk and Room Conversation --
December 26, 1976, Bombay   133
- Room Conversation -- December 26, 1976,
Bombay   134
- Press Interview -- December 31, 1976,
Bombay   135
- Evening Conversation -- January 25,
1977, Puri   136
- Room Conversation -- February 3, 1977,
Bhuvanesvara   136
- Room Conversation -- February 14, 1977,
Mayapura   137
- Room Conversation -- March 22, 1977,
Bombay   138
- Room Conversation with Ratan Singh
Rajda (Member of Parliament) -- March 27,
1977, Bombay   139
- Interview with Mr. Koshi (Asst. Editor of
The Current Weekly) -- April 5, 1977,
Bombay   139
- Morning Talk -- April 5, 1977, Bombay   140
- Room Conversation with Ratan Singh
Rajda M.P. 'Nationalism and Cheating' --
April 15, 1977, Bombay   140
- Room Conversation Meeting with Dr.
Sharma (from Russia) -- April 17, 1977,
Bombay   142
- Second Meeting with Mr. Dwivedi -- April
24, 1977, Bombay   143
- Evening Darsana -- May 12, 1977,
Hrishikesh   143

- Room Conversation with Sri Narayana and
Rama-Krsna Bajaj -- October 31, 1977,
Vrndavana   144

-An Address given in Bombay late 1960s   145

20. CLOSING STATEMENT   147

About the Compiler   149

VERSES AND OTHER REFERENCES   151

His Divine Grace A.C.Bhaktivedanta Swami Prabhupada
Founder Acharya of International Society
for Krishna Consciousness

Describing the glories and fortune of taking birth as human beings in Bharata-varsha (India and Earth) As Instructed by Sri Chaitanya MahaPrabhu

bhārata-bhūmite haila manuṣya-janma yāra
janma sārthaka kari' kara para-upakāra

"One who has taken his birth as a human being in the land of India [Bhārata-varṣa] should make his life successful and work for the benefit of all other people.

"Anyone who has taken birth as a human being in India Bharata-Bhumi"

—Mangalacarana—
nama om visnu-padaya krsna prestaya bhutale
srimate bhaktivedanta swami iti namine
namas te savasvate deve gaura vani-pracharine
nirvisesa sunyavadi pascatya-desa-tarine

I offer my humble obeisance, unto you, my beloved spiritual master, His Divine Grace Om Vishnupada Paramahamsa Parivrajakacharya Astottara Sata Sri Srimad A. C. Bhakivedanta Swami Maharaja Srila Prabhupada, who is extremely dear to Sri Krsna, having taken shelter at His lotus feet.

Our respectful obeisance's unto you, O servant of Srila Bhaktisiddhanti Sarasvati Thakura Prabhupada. You are kindly preaching the message of Sri Gaurasundara and delivering the Western countries that are filled with impersonalism and voidism.

panca-tattvatmakam krsnam bhakta-rupa-svarupakam
bhaktavataram bhaktakhyam namami bhakta-saktikam
sri krsna-caitanya prabhu-nityananda
sri advaita gadadhara srivasadi-gaura-bhakta-vrnda

I offer obeisances unto Sri Krsna Caitanya Mahaprabhu in His five features as bhakta-rupa Sri Caitanya Mahaprabhu, bhakta-svarupa Nityananda Prabhu, bhakta-avatara Sri Advaita Acarya, bhakta-sakti Sri Gadadhara Pandita, Bhakta Srivasa, and to all of the devotees of Sri Gauranga.

Hare Krishna Hare Krishna
Krishna Krishna Hare Hare
Hare Rama Hare Rama
Rama Rama Hare Hare

DEDICATION

There are no words to express properly how grateful I am to our beloved spiritual master, nitya-lila-pravista om vishnupada paramahamsa parivrajakacarya astottara-sata Sri Srimad His Divine Grace A. C. Bhaktivedanta Swami Maharaja Srila Prabhupada—to whom I will always be eternally indebted.

I pray at His lotus feet, who has been too kind to me and is the inspiration behind this project, hoping He will be pleased.

My vartma-pradarshaka guru, His Grace Sriman Balaka das Prabhu, whose guidance and encouragement inspired me to take shelter of our beloved spiritual master.

Sriman Raghunandana das Prabhu, my maternal-paternal brother and most significant godbrother who encouraged me to go and hear the words of Sriman Balaka das Prabhu during the early days (1970's) in our home town "Riggs-Park" Washington D.C.

To my parents, without whom the opportunity in this lifetime would not have taken place.

To all my god-brothers/sisters and all the dedicated book distributors of Srila Prabhupada's transcendental literature, serving Srila Prabhupada's mission.

"Whenever I get a report of my book selling, I feel strength. Even now, in this weakened condition, I have got strength from your report. You should know that in this work you have Krishna's Blessings." Letter to Satsvarupa 9/8/1974.

"Whatever progress we have made, it is simply due to distributing the books. So go on, and do not divert your mind for a moment from this." Letter to Ramesvara 10/11/1974.

PREFACE

When Srila Prabhupada returned to India with his "White Elephants" (newly initiated Western disciples) from his initial embarkment to America in 1965, crowds gathered wherever he went as he preached his epiphanic message to his fellow Indian compatriots Lord Sri Chaitanya MahaPrabhu's Instructions:

bharata bhumite haila manusya janma yara
janma sarthaka kari' kara para-upakara

"Having taken a human birth in Bharata-varsha (India), make your life successful by preaching this transcendental message of Krishna consciousness to the world."

Examining that same *Srimad-Bhagavatam* that Lord Brahma read more than three times himself, and having heard lectures spoken from Srila Prabhupada so many times also, Shambhu dasa, a formally initiated disciple of Srila Prabhupada, became inspired by two essential, recurring themes in Srila Prabhupada's books: First, the importance of attaining a human birth and utilizing it properly, and secondly, the immense *sukrti* or pious credits by taking birth in Bharata-varsha or India and its subsequent opportunities. Although Srila Prabhupada's causeless mercy from his own spiritual master brought him to the Western shores of a bustling, chaotic New York City in the mid-60s for preaching his spiritual master's message, his satisfied heart still yearned for his true home in Sri Vrindavana Dhama, the birthplace of Lord Krishna. His self-determination of spreading this vital message led him to a successful life, both here and for eternity. Srila Prabhupada took that prabhu-*desha* -order to heart, travelled to America, and finally Krishna empowered him to establish the divine, personal connection of *bhakti-yoga* and spread this panacea all over the world.

Throughout this book Shambhu Prabhu presents and highlights some great "Jewels" of Instructions given by Srila Prabhupada and the various scriptures (shastra) that will surely encourage any reader to see how fortunate they are granted this rare life as a human being, whether In India Bharat-varsha or anywhere on this planet (Earth).

We can only try to follow in his footsteps and pray that our attempts will be successful, as he stressed throughout his life and teachings.

Dasanudasa
Tirthapada

INTRODUCTION

For Many Years During The Summer Months, I would get together with a few intimate devotee friends, *guru-bhais* (Godbrothers), and associates. It was a great program, coming from all across the country and the world to discuss (*sat-sanga*) and study various *shastras* or Vedic scriptures. I was impressed with the number of verses specifically relating to the "fortune" of "human beings" taking birth in Bharata-varsha (India, planet-earth). This inspired me to expand upon the topic a bit more. Although I did not start out with a mindset to come up with a sizeable booklet; it took its own shape and was encouraged to continue—as a result, we are here now. It was suggested to use a direct quote from Srila Prabhupada for the title—the significance of his quote would give even more relevance to the subjects of the book as well.

I have only scratched the surface from our guru-parampara and Srila Prabhupada's teachings on this subject. Here's one small attempt to help one see and understand their fortune as human beings.

Most of the information is derived from Srila Prabhupada's translated books: *Srimad-Bhagavatam, Sri Caitanya-Carita-mrta, Bhagavad-Gita As It Is,* lectures, morning walks, purports, addresses and so on. These two quotes, I felt, were perfect since the subjects are contained within them.

"Anyone Who Has Taken Birth As A Human Being In India - Bharata-Bhumi" and "Not The Cats And Dogs But Those Who Have Taken Human Form"

As an artist-musician and songwriter, generally the "Title" of the song is the subject matter of which the song is about. Using a similar format in this endeavor helped me to stay focused on the subject at hand.

Originally, it was to be into two parts, then decided to stick with the theme of the before mentioned format and instead of two parts in one book.

Have a follow-up book using the second title, which covers how fortunate living entities taking birth as human beings and the duty with such fortune.

This book will cover human beings who have taken birth in Bharata-Bhumi, India (Earth).

As described in the Vedic literature (Bhagavad Gita As It Is) that there are four different Ages that continuously come and go like the four seasons or calendar months in a year, namely described as Satya, Treta, Dvapara and Kali-yuga.

Our present Age is Kali-yuga. In order to get a glimpse and start the process of understanding the fortune for anyone awarded the human form of life in this Age, what to speak of Bharata-varsha (present day India).

One **important point** to be made, as stated in the *Srimad-Bhagavatam* and other Vedic literature, Bharata-varsha is also referred to as the planet earth. It is part of the larger island of Jambudvipa, the center of Bhu-mandala, situated in the middle planetary system within this universe. So, Bharat-varsha will also be referred to this planet earth.

Shambhu dasa

Acknowledgments

I am truly grateful to my godbrothers, sisters for advising and pushing me to finish this book, Tirthapada das Prabhu chief editor, Adridharana das Prabhu for providing valuable advice and information, Bhumipati das, Bhakta Jeffery Prabhu's helping to keep the computer running, Shankara Pandita das, Sanatana Goswami das, Bhaktivenode das Prabhu's encouragement and unwavering help.

Ms. Sharee Brown "Sridevi" the graphics, professional input has set the tone which helped the project to move forward and get finished in a timely fashion. The selfless support given me for so many years to be thankful can never be stressed enough. I pray for your continued "Blessings" from the Lord and His devotees.

SRI ISOPANISHAD
TEXT 3

Starting from Sri-Isopanishad

asuryā nāma te lokā, andhena tamasāvrtāh
tāms te pretyābhigacchanti, ye ke cātma-hano janāh

TRANSLATION

The killer of the soul, whoever he may be, must enter into the planets known as the worlds of the faithless, full of darkness and ignorance.

(*Sri Isopanishad* 3)

PURPORT

Human life is distinguished from animal life due to its heavy responsibilities. Those who are cognizant of these responsibilities and who work in that spirit are called *suras* (godly persons), and those who are neglectful of these responsibilities or who have no information about them are called *asuras* (demons). Throughout the universe, there are only these two types of human beings. In the Ṛg Veda, it is stated that the *suras* always aim at the lotus feet of the Supreme Lord Viṣ-nu and act accordingly. Their ways are as illuminated as the path of the sun.

Intelligent human beings must always remember that the soul obtains a human form after an evolution of many millions of years in the cycle of transmigration. The material world is sometimes compared to an ocean, and the human body is compared to a solid boat designed especially to cross this ocean. The Vedic scriptures and the *ācāryas*, or saintly teachers, are compared to expert boatmen, and the facilities of the human body are compared to favorable breezes that help the boat ply smoothly to its desired destination. If with all these facilities, a human being does not fully utilize his life for self-realization, he must be considered *ātma-hā*, a killer of the soul. *Śrī Īśopaniṣad* warns in clear terms that the killer of the soul is destined to enter into the darkest region of ignorance to suffer perpetually.

There are swine, dogs, camels, asses, etc., whose economic necessities are just as important to them as ours are to us, but the economic problems of these animals are solved only under nasty and unpleasant conditions. The human being is given all facilities for a comfortable life by the laws of nature because the human form of life is more important and valuable than animal life. Why is man given a better life than that of the swine and other animals? Why is a highly placed government servant given better facilities than those of an ordinary clerk?

The answer is that a highly placed officer has to discharge duties of a higher nature. Similarly, the duties human beings have to perform are higher than those of animals, who are always engaged in simply feeding their hungry stomachs. Yet the modern soul-killing civilization has only increased the problems of the hungry stomach. When we approach a polished animal in the form of a modern civilized man and ask him to take an interest in self-realization, he will say that he simply wants to work to satisfy his stomach and that there is no need for self-realization for a hungry man. The laws of nature are so cruel, however, that despite his denunciation of the need for self-realization and his eagerness to work hard to fill his stomach, he is always threatened by unemployment.

We are given this human form of life not to work hard like asses, swine and dogs but to attain the highest perfection of life. If we do not care for self-realization, the laws of nature force us to work very hard, even though we may not want to do so. Human beings in this age have been forced to work hard like the asses and bullocks that pull carts. Some of the regions where the asuras are sent to work are revealed in this verse of Śrī Īśopaniṣad. If a man fails to discharge his duties as a human being, he is forced to transmigrate to the asurya planets and take birth to degraded species of life to work hard in ignorance and darkness.

In the *Bhagavad-gītā* (6.41-43) it is stated that a man who enters upon the path of self-realization but does not complete the process, despite having sincerely tried to realize his relationship with God, is given a chance to appear in a family of *śuci* or *śrīmat*. The word śuci indicates a spiritually advanced brāhmana, and śrīmat indicates a vaiśya, a member of the mercantile community. So, the person who fails to achieve self-realization is given a better chance in his next life due to his sincere efforts in this life. If even a fallen candidate is given a chance to take birth in a respectable and noble family, one can hardly imagine the status of one who has achieved success. By simply attempting to realize God, one is guaranteed birth in a wealthy or aristocratic family. But those who do not even make an attempt, who wants to be covered by illusion, who are too materialistic and too attached to material enjoyment, must enter into the darkest regions of hell, as confirmed throughout the Vedic literature.

Such materialistic *asuras* sometimes make a show of religion, but their ultimate aim is material prosperity. The *Bhagavad-gītā* (16.17-18) rebukes such men by calling them *ātma-sambhāvita*, meaning that they are considered great only on the strength of deception and are empowered by the votes of the ignorant and by their own material wealth. Such *asuras*, devoid of self-realization and knowledge of *īśāvāsya*, the Lord's universal proprietorship, are certain to enter into the darkest regions.

The verses Srila Prabhupada mentioned previously from the *Bhagavad-Gita As It Is,* are 6.41, 42, 43:

> *prāpya punya-krtām lokān usitvā śāśvatīh samāh*
> *śucīnām śrīmatām gehe yoga-bhrasto 'bhijāyate*

> *atha vā yoginām eva kule bhavati dhīmatām*
> *etad dhi durlabha-taram loke janma yad īdrśam*

tatra tam buddhi-samyogam labhate paurva-dehikam
yatate ca tato bhūyah samsiddhau kuru-nandana

The unsuccessful yogi, after many, many years of enjoyment on the planets of the pious living entities, is born into a family of righteous people, or into a family of rich aristocracy.

Or if unsuccessful after long practice of yoga, he takes his birth in a family of transcendentalists who are surely great in wisdom. Certainly, such a birth is rare in this world.

On taking such a birth, he revives the divine consciousness of his previous life, and he again tries to make further progress in order to achieve complete success, O son of Kuru.

The conclusion is that as human beings, we are meant not simply for solving economic problems on a tottering platform but for solving all the problems of the material life into which we have been placed by the laws of nature.

SRIMAD-BHAGAVATAM
CANTO 4 CHAPTER 23 TEXT 28

स वञ्चितो बतात्मध्रुक् कृच्छ्रेण महता भुवि ।
लब्ध्वापवर्ग्यं मानुष्यं विषयेषु विषज्जते ॥ २८ ॥

sa vañcito batātma-dhruk, kṛcchrena mahatā bhuvi
labdhvāpavargyam mānusyam, visayesu visajjate

TRANSLATION

Any person who engages himself within this material world in performing activities that necessitate great struggle, and who, after obtaining a human form of life—which is a chance to attain liberation from miseries—undertakes the difficult tasks of fruitive activities, must be considered to be cheated and envious of his own self.

(Srimad-Bhagavatam 4.23.28)

Purport

In this material world, people are engaged in different activities simply to achieve a little success in sense gratification. The *karmīs* are engaged in performing very difficult activities, and thus they open gigantic factories, build huge cities, make big scientific discoveries, etc. In other words, they are engaged in performing very costly sacrifices in order to be promoted to the higher planetary systems. Similarly, *yogīs* are engaged in achieving a similar goal by accepting the tedious practices of mystic yoga. *Jñānīs* are engaged in philosophical speculation in order to gain release from the clutches of material nature. In these ways everyone is engaged in performing very difficult tasks simply for the gratification of the senses. All of these are considered to be engaged in sense gratificatory activities (*viṣaya*) because they all demand some facility for material existence. Actually, the results of such activities are temporary. As Krsna Himself proclaims in *Bhagavad-Gita* 7.23, antavat tu phalam tesām: "The fruits of those who worship the demigods are limited and temporary." Thus, the fruits of the activities of the yogis, karmīs and jñānīs are ephemeral.

Moreover, Krsna says, *tad bhavaty alpa-medhasām*: "They are simply meant for men of small intelligence." The word *viṣaya* denotes sense gratification. The *karmīs* flatly state that they want sense gratification. The *yogīs* also want sense gratification, but they want it to a higher degree. It is their desire to show some miraculous results through the practice of yoga. Thus, they strive very hard to achieve success in becoming smaller than the smallest or greater than the greatest, or in creating a planet like earth or, as scientists, by inventing so many wonderful machines. Similarly, the *jñānīs* are also engaged in sense gratification, for they are simply interested in becoming one with the Supreme.

Thus, the aim of all these activities is to sense gratification to a higher or a lower degree. The *bhaktas,* however, are not interested in sense gratificatory practices; they are simply satisfied to get an opportunity to serve the Lord. Although they are satisfied in any condition, there is nothing they cannot obtain, because they are purely engaged in the service of the Lord.

The wives of the demigods condemn the performers of sense gratificatory activities as vañcita, cheated. Those so engaged are actually killing themselves (*ātma-hā*). As stated in *Srimad-Bhagavatam* (11.12.27):

> *nr-deham ādyam sulabham sudurlabham*
> *plavam sukalpam guru-karnadhāram*
> *mayānukūlena nabhasvateritam*
> *pumān bhavābdhim na taret sa ātma-hā*

When one wants to cross a large ocean, he requires a strong boat. It is said that this human form of life is a good boat by which one can cross the ocean of nescience. In the human form of life one can obtain the guidance of a good navigator, the spiritual master. One also gets a favorable wind by the mercy of Krsna, and that wind is the instructions of Krsna. The human body is the boat, the instructions of Lord Krsna are the favorable winds, and the spiritual master is the navigator. The spiritual master knows well how to adjust the sails to catch the winds favorably and steer the boat to its destination. If, however, one does not take advantage of this opportunity, one wastes the human form of life. Wasting time and life in this way is the same as committing suicide.

The word *labdhvāpavargyam* is significant in this verse because, according to Jīva Gosvāmī, *āpavargyam*, or the path of liberation, does not refer to merging into the impersonal Brahman but to *sālokyādi-siddhi*, which means attaining the very planet where the Supreme Personality of Godhead resides. There are five kinds of liberation, and one is called *sāyujya-mukti*, or merging into the existence of the Supreme, or the impersonal Brahman effulgence. However, since there is a chance of one's falling down again into the material sky from the Brahman effulgence, Śrīla Jīva Gosvāmī advises that in this human form of life, one's only aim should be to go back home, back to Godhead. The words *sa vañcitah* indicate that once a person has obtained the human form of life, he is actually cheated if he does not make preparations to go back home, back to Godhead. The position of all non-devotees, who are not interested in going back to Godhead, is very much lamentable, for the human form of life is meant for executing devotional service and nothing else.

CONVERSATION DR. BENFORD

Here's a conversation where the living-entities (souls) bodily transmigration explained taken from "The Journey of Self Discovery"- His Divine Grace A.C. Bhaktivedanta Swami Prabhupada with Dr. Benford.

Dr. Benford: How do you know that people return in some other form?

Śrīla Prabhupāda said: We see that there are so many forms. Where do these different forms come from -- the form of the dog, the form of the cat, the form of the tree, the form of the reptile, the forms of the insects, the forms of the fish? What is your explanation for all these different forms? That you do not know.

Dr. Benford: Evolution.

Śrīla Prabhupāda said: Not exactly. The different species are already existing. "Fish," "tiger," "man" -- all of these are already existing. It is just like the different types of apartments here in Los Angeles. You may occupy one of them according to your ability to pay rent, but all types of apartments are nevertheless existing at the same time. Similarly, the living entity, according to his karma, is given facility to occupy one of these bodily forms. But there is evolution, also -- spiritual evolution. From the fish, the soul evolves to plant life. From plant forms the living entity enters an insect body. From the insect body the next stage is bird, then beast, and finally the spirit soul may evolve to the human form of life. And from the human form, if one becomes qualified, he may evolve further. Otherwise, he must again enter the evolutionary cycle. **Therefore, this human form of life is an important juncture in the evolutionary development of the living entity.**

In the Bhāgavad Gītā: 9:25 Krsna says,

yanti deva-vrata devan pitrn yanti pitr-vratah
bhutani yanti bhutejya yanti mad-yajino 'pi mam

In other words, whatever you like you can achieve. There are different lokas, or planetary systems, and you can go to the higher planetary systems where the demigods live and take a body there, or you can go where the Pitas, or ancestors, live. You can take a body here in Bhuloka, the earthly planetary system, or you can go to the planet of God, Krsnaloka. This method of transferring oneself at the time of death to whatever planet one chooses is called yoga. There is a physical process of yoga, a philosophical process of yoga, and a devotional process of yoga. The devotees can go directly to planet where Krsna is.

SRIMAD-BHAGAVATAM
CANTO 7 CHAPTER 6 TEXT 1

Next taken from Srimad-Bhagavatam, Sri Prahlada Maharaja, one of the great Mahajanas (great authorities of the Vedic literature), instructs one who is fortunate to have the human form.

श्रीप्रह्लाद उवाच
कौमार आचरेत्प्राज्ञो धर्मान्भागवतानिह ।
दुर्लभं मानुषं जन्म तदप्यध्रुवमर्थदम् ॥

śrī-prahrāda uvāca
kaumāra ācaret prājño dharmān bhāgavatān iha
durlabham mānusam janma tad apy adhruvam arthadam

TRANSLATION

Prahlāda Mahārāja said: One who is sufficiently intelligent should use the human form of body from the

very beginning of life—in other words, from the tender age of childhood—to practice the activities of devotional service, giving up all other engagements. The human body is most rarely achieved, and although temporary like other bodies, it is meaningful because in human life, one can perform devotional service. Even a slight amount of sincere devotional service can give one complete perfection.

(*Srimad-Bhagavatam* 7.6.1)

PURPORT

The whole purpose of Vedic civilization and of reading the Vedas is to attain the perfect stage of devotional service in the human form of life. According to the Vedic system, therefore, from the very beginning of life, the brahmacarya system is introduced so that from one's very childhood—from the age of five years—one can practice modifying one's human activities so as to engage perfectly in devotional service. As confirmed in *Bhagavad-gītā* (2.40), *svalpam apy asya dharmasya trāyate mahato bhayāt*: "Even a little advancement on this path can protect one from the most dangerous type of fear." Modern civilization, not referring to the verdicts of Vedic literature, is so cruel to the members of human society that instead of teaching children to become brahmacārīs, it teaches mothers to kill their children even in the womb, in the plea of curbing the increase of population. And if by chance a child is saved, he is educated only for sense gratification. Gradually, throughout the entire world, human society is losing interest in the perfection of life. Indeed, men are living like cats and dogs, spoiling the duration of their human lives by actually preparing to transmigrate again to the degraded species among the 8,400,000 forms of life. The Krsna consciousness movement is anxious to serve human society by teaching people to perform devotional service, which can save a human being from being degraded again to animal life. As already stated by Prahlāda Mahārāja, *bhāgavata-dharma* consists of *sravanah kīrtanah visnoh smaranam pāda-sevanam/ arcanam vandanam dāsyam sakhyam ātma-nivedanam*. In all the schools, colleges and universities, and at home, all children and youths should be taught to hear about the Supreme Personality of Godhead. In other words, they should be taught to hear the instructions of *Bhagavad-gītā*, to put them into practice in their lives, and thus become strong in devotional service, free from fear of being degraded to animal life. Following *bhāgavata-dharma* has been made extremely easy in this Age of Kali.

The *sāstra* says:

> *harer nāma harer nāma harer nāmaiva kevalam*
> *kalau nāsty eva nāsty eva nāsty eva gatir anyathā*

One need only chant the Hare Krsna mahā-mantra. Everyone engaged in the practice of chanting the Hare Krsna *mahā-mantra* will be completely cleansed, from the core of his heart, and be saved from the cycle of birth and death.

———

Here verse Bhagavad-Gita-as It Is-2.40 mentioned in purport above

नेहाभिक्रमनाशोऽस्ति प्रत्यवायो न विद्यते ।
स्वल्पमप्यस्य धर्मस्य त्रायते महतो भयात् ॥ ४० ॥

nehābhikrama-nāśo 'sti pratyavāyo na vidyate
sv-alpam apy asya dharmasya trāyate mahato bhayāt

TRANSLATION

In this endeavor, there is no loss or diminution, and a little advancement on this path can protect one from the most dangerous type of fear.

PURPORT

Activity in Kṛṣṇa consciousness, or acting for the benefit of Kṛṣṇa without expectation of sense gratification, is the highest transcendental quality of work. Even a small beginning of such activity finds no impediment, nor can that small beginning be lost at any stage. Any work begun on the material plane has to be completed. Otherwise, the whole attempt becomes a failure. But any work begun in Kṛṣṇa consciousness has a permanent effect, even though not finished. The performer of such work is therefore not at a loss even if his work in Kṛṣṇa consciousness is incomplete. One percent done in Kṛṣṇa consciousness bears permanent results, so that the next beginning is from the point of two percent, whereas in material activity without a hundred percent success, there is no profit. Ajāmila performed his duty in some percentage of Kṛṣṇa consciousness, but the result he enjoyed at the end was a hundred percent, by the grace of the Lord. There is a nice verse in this connection in *Śrīmad-Bhāgavatam* (1.5.17):

tyaktvā sva-dharmaṁ caraṇāmbujaṁ harer
bhajann apakvo 'tha patet tato yadi

yatra kva vābhadram abhūd amuṣya kiṁ
ko vārtha āpto 'bhajatāṁ sva-dharmataḥ

"If someone gives up his occupational duties and works in Kṛṣṇa consciousness and then falls down on account of not completing his work, what loss is there on his part? And what can one gain if one performs his material activities perfectly?" Or, as the Christians say, "What profiteth a man if he gains the whole world yet suffers the loss of his eternal soul?"

Material activities and their results end with the body. But work in Kṛṣṇa consciousness carries a person again to Kṛṣṇa consciousness, even after the loss of the body. At least one is sure to have a chance in the next life of being born again as a human being, either in the family of a great cultured *brāh-maṇa* or in a rich aristocratic family that will give one a further chance for elevation. That is the unique quality of work done in Kṛṣṇa consciousness.

Srimad Bhagavatam

Canto 7 Chapter 6 Text 2

यथा हि पुरुषस्येह विष्णो: पादोपसर्पणम् ।
यदेष सर्वभूतानां प्रिय आत्मेश्वर: सुहृत् ॥ २ ॥

yathā hi purusasyeha visnoh pādopasarpanam
yad esa sarva-bhūtānām priya ātmeśvarah suhrt

Translation

The human form of life affords one a chance to return home, back to Godhead. Therefore, every living entity, especially in the human form of life, must engage in devotional service to the lotus feet of Lord Visnu. This devotional service is natural because Lord Visnu, the Supreme Personality of Godhead, is the most beloved, the master of the soul, and the well-wisher of all other living beings.

(Srimad-Bhagavatam 7-6-2)

Purport

The Lord says in *Bhagavad-gītā (5.29)*:

bhoktāram yajña-tapasām sarva-loka-maheśvaram
suhrdam sarva-bhūtānām jñātvā mām śāntim rcchati

"The sage who knows Me as the ultimate purpose of all sacrifices and austerities, the Supreme Lord of all planets and demigods and the benefactor and well-wisher of all living entities attains peace from the pangs of material miseries." Simply by understanding these three facts—that the Supreme Lord, Visnu, is the proprietor of the entire creation, that He is the best well-wishing friend of all living entities, and that He is the supreme enjoyer of everything—one becomes peaceful and happy. For this transcendental happiness, the living entity has wandered throughout the universe in different forms of life and different planetary systems, but because he has forgotten his intimate relationship with Visnu, he has merely suffered, life after life. Therefore, the educational system in the human form of life should be so perfect that one will understand his intimate relationship with God, or Visnu. Every living entity has an intimate relationship with God. One should therefore glorify the Lord in the adoration of śānta-rasa or revive his eternal relationship with Visnu as a servant in dāsya-rasa, a friend in sakhya-rasa, a parent in vātsalya-rasa or a conjugal lover in mādhurya-rasa. All these relationships are on the platform of love. Visnu is the center of love for everyone, and therefore the duty of everyone is to engage in the loving service of the Lord. As stated by the Supreme Personality of Godhead (Bhāg. 3.25.38), yesām aham priya ātmā sutaś ca sakhā guruh suhrdo daivam istam. In any form of life, we are related with Visnu, who is the most beloved, the Supersoul, son, friend, and guru. Our eternal relationship with God can be revived in the human form of life, and that should be the goal of education. Indeed, that is the perfection of life and the perfection of education.

Srimad Bhagavatam

कुटुम्बपोषाय वियन्निजायु
र्न बुध्यतेऽर्थं विहतं प्रमत्तः ।
सर्वत्र तापत्रयदुः खितात्मा
निर्विद्यते न स्वकुटुम्बरामः ॥ १४ ॥

kuṭumba-poṣāya viyan nijāyur na budhyate 'rthaṁ
vihataṁ pramattaḥ
sarvatra tāpa-traya-duḥkhitātmā nirvidyate
na sva-kuṭumba-rāmaḥ

Translation

One who is too attached cannot understand that he is wasting his valuable life for the maintenance of his family. He also fails to understand that the purpose of human life, a life suitable for realization of the Absolute Truth, is being imperceptibly spoiled. However, he is very cleverly attentive to seeing that not a single farthing

is lost by mismanagement. Thus, although an attached person in material existence always suffers from three-fold miseries, he does not develop a distaste for the way of material existence.

(Srimad-Bhagavatam 7-6-14)

Purport

A foolish man does not understand the values of human life, nor does he understand how he is wasting his valuable life simply for the maintenance of his family members. He is an expert in calculating the loss of pounds, shillings and pence, but he is so foolish that he does not know how much money he is losing, even according to material considerations. Cānakya Pandita gives the example that a moment of life cannot be purchased in exchange for millions of dollars. A foolish person, however, wastes such a valuable life without knowing how much he is losing, even according to monetary calculations. Although a materialistic person is an expert in calculating costs and doing business, he does not realize that he is misusing his costly life for want of knowledge. Even though such a materialistic person is always suffering threefold miseries, he is not intelligent enough to cease his materialistic way of life.

Srimad Bhagavatam

Canto 7 Chapter 6 Text 15

वित्तेषु नित्याभिनिविष्टचेता
विद्वांश्च दोषं परवित्तहर्तुः ।
प्रेत्येह वाथाप्यजितेन्द्रियस्त-
दशान्तकामो हरते कुटुम्बी ॥ १५ ॥

vitteṣu nityābhiniviṣṭa-cetā vidvāṁś ca doṣaṁ
para-vitta-hartuḥ
pretyeha vāthapy ajitendriyas tad aśānta-kāmo
harate kuṭumbī

Translation

If a person too attached to the duties of family maintenance is unable to control his senses, the core of his heart is immersed in how to accumulate money. Although he knows that one who takes the wealth of others will be punished by the law of the government

and by the laws of Yamarāja after death, he continues cheating others to acquire money.

Srimad-Bhagavatam 7-6-15

PURPORT

Especially these days, people do not believe in the next life or in the court of Yamarāja and the various punishments of the sinful. But at least one should know that one who cheats on others to acquire money will be punished by the laws of the government. Nonetheless, people do not care about the laws of this life or those governing the next. Despite whatever knowledge one has, one cannot stop his sinful activities if he is unable to control his senses.

SECTARIANISM

(*Science of Self-Realization,* page 105)

"There is a misconception that the Krishna consciousness movement represents the Hindu religion. In fact, however, Krishna consciousness is in no way a faith or religion that seeks to defeat other faiths or religions. Rather, it is an essential cultural movement for the entire human society and does not consider any particular sectarian faith. This cultural movement is especially meant to educate people in how they can love God. Sometimes Indians, both inside and outside of India, think that we are preaching the Hindu religion, but actually, we are not. One will not find the word "Hindu" in the Bhagavad-Gita. Indeed, there is no such word as Hindu" in the entire Vedic literature. This word has been introduced by Baluchistan, the Muslims from provinces next to India, such as Afghanistan, and Persia. There is a river called Sindhu bordering the north-western provinces of India, and since the Muslims there could not pronounce Sindhu properly, they instead called the river "Hindu," and the inhabitants of this tract of land they called "Hindus."

Sectarianism

"Sectarianism is a natural byproduct of the Absolute Truth. When *ācāryas* first ascertain and instruct the Truth, it is not polluted with sectarianism. But the rules and regulations received through disciplic succession regarding the goal and the method of achieving it are changed in due course of time according to the mentality and locale of the people

> *yathā-prakṛti sarveṣāṁ citrā vācaḥ sravanti hi*
> *evaṁ prakṛti-vaicitryād bhidyante matayo nṛṇām*
> *pāramparyeṇa keṣāñcit pāṣaṇḍa-matayo 'pare*

"Therefore, because of the different characteristics of the living entities within the universe, there are a great many Vedic rituals, mantras, and rewards. Due to the great variety of desires and natures among human beings, there are many different theistic philosophies of life, which are handed down through tradition, custom, and disciplic succession. There are other teachers who directly support atheistic viewpoints." (*Bhāg.* 11.14.7-8)

A rule that is followed by one society is not necessarily accepted in another society. That is why one community is different from another. As a community gradually develops more respect for its own standards, it develops hatred towards other communities and considers their standards inferior.

These sectarian symptoms are seen in all countries since time immemorial."

This is taken from Srila Bhaktivinoda Thakur's introduction of his composition Sri Krishna Samhita:

We learn how the sectarian mentality has progressed throughout human society which seems to be a never-ending progression, and this mentality has no boundaries when it comes to Sanatana-Dharma mentioned next.

Sanatana Dharma

**Srimad Bhagavatam
Canto 6 Chapter 16 Text 41**

विषममतिर्न यत्र नृणां
त्वमहमिति मम तवेति च यदन्यत्र ।
विषमधिया रचितो यः
स ह्याविशुद्धः क्षयिष्णुरधर्मबहुलः ॥ ४१ ॥

viṣama-matir na yatra nṛṇāṁ tvam *aham iti mama taveti
ca yad anyatra
viṣama-dhiyā racito yaḥ* sa *hy aviśuddhaḥ kṣayiṣṇur adharma-
bahulaḥ*

Translation

Being full of contradictions, all forms of religion but *Bhagavata-dharma* work under conceptions of fruitive results and distinctions of "you and I" and "yours and mine." The followers of Śrīmad-Bhāgavatam have no such consciousness. They are all Kṛṣṇa conscious, thinking that they are Kṛṣṇa's and Kṛṣṇa is theirs. There are other low-class religious systems, which are contemplated for the killing of enemies or the gain of mystic power, but such religious systems, being full of passion and envy, are impure and temporary. Because they are full of envy, they are full of irreligion.

(SB-Canto-6-Ch-16-text-41)

Purport

Bhāgavata-dharma has no contradictions. Conceptions of "your religion" and "my religion" are completely absent from *bhāgavata-dharma*. *Bhāgavata-dharma* means following the orders given by the Supreme Lord, Bhagavān, as stated in *Bhagavad-gītā: sarva-dharmān parityajya mām ekaṁ śaraṇaṁ vraja.* God is one, and God is for everyone. Therefore, everyone must surrender to God. That is the pure conception of religion. Whatever God orders constitutes religion (*dharmaṁ tu sākṣād bhagavat-praṇītam*). In *bhāgavata-dharma* there is no question of "what you believe" and "what I believe." Everyone must believe in the Supreme Lord and carry out His orders. *Ānukūlyena kṛṣṇānuśīlanam:* whatever

Kṛṣṇa says — whatever God says — should be directly carried out. That is *dharma,* religion.

If one is actually Kṛṣṇa conscious, he cannot have any enemies. Since his only engagement is to induce others to surrender to Kṛṣṇa, or God, how can he have enemies? If one advocates the Hindu religion, the Muslim religion, the Christian religion, this religion, or that religion, there will be conflicts. History shows that the followers of religious systems without a clear conception of God have fought with one another. There are many instances of this in human history, but systems of religion that do not concentrate upon service to the Supreme are temporary and cannot last for long because they are full of envy. There are many activities directed against such religious systems, and therefore one must give up the idea of "my belief" and "your belief." Everyone should believe in God and surrender unto Him. That is *bhāgavata-dharma.*

Bhāgavata-dharma is not a concocted sectarian belief, for it entails research to find how everything is connected with Kṛṣṇa (*īśāvāsyam idaṁ sarvam*). According to the Vedic injunctions, *sarvaṁ khalv idaṁ brahma:* "Brahman, the Supreme, is present in everything." *Bhāgavata-dharma* captures this presence of the Supreme. *Bhāgavata-dharma* does not consider everything in the world to be false. Because everything emanates from the Supreme, nothing can be false. Everything has some use in the service of the Supreme. For example, we are now dictating into a microphone and recording on a dictating machine, and thus we are finding how the machine can be connected to the Supreme Brahman. Since we are using this machine in the service of the Lord, it is Brahman.

This is the meaning of *sarvaṁ khalv idaṁ brahma.* Everything is Brahman because everything can be used for the service of the Supreme Lord. Nothing is *mithyā,* false; everything is factual.

Bhāgavata-dharma is called *sarvotkṛṣṭa,* the best of all religious systems, because those who follow *bhāgavata-dharma* are not envious of anyone. Pure *bhāgavatas,* pure devotees, invite everyone, without envy, to join the Kṛṣṇa consciousness movement. A devotee is, therefore, exactly like the Supreme Personality of Godhead. *Suhṛdaṁ sarva-bhūtānām:* he is the friend of all living entities. Therefore, this is the best of all religious systems. Whereas so-called religions are meant for a particular type of person who believes in a particular way, such discrimination has no place in Kṛṣṇa consciousness, or *bhāgavata-dharma.* If we scrutinize the religious systems meant for worship of demigods or anyone else but the Supreme Personality of Godhead, we will find that they are full of envy and therefore impure.

Sanatana Dharma

"SANATANA-DHARMA" The "souls-eternal-occupational-duty"

Srila Prabhupada: In the Introduction of Bhagavad-Gita As It Is

"*Sanātana-dharma* does not refer to any sectarian process of religion. It is the eternal function of the eternal living entities in relationship with the eternal Supreme Lord. *Sanātana-dharma* refers, as stated previously, to the eternal occupation of the living entity. Śrīpāda Rāmānujācārya has explained the word *sanātana* as "that which has neither beginning nor end," so when we speak of *sanātana-dharma,* we must take it for granted on the authority of Śrīpāda Rāmānujācārya that it has neither beginning nor end.

"The English word "religion" is a little different from *sanātana-dharma.* Religion conveys the idea of faith, and faith may change. One may have faith in a particular process, and he may change this faith and adopt another, but *sanātana-dharma* refers to that activity which cannot be changed. For instance, liquidity cannot be taken from water, nor can heat be taken from fire. Similarly, the eternal function of the eternal living entity cannot be taken from the living entity. *Sanātana-dharma* is eternally integral with the living entity. When we speak of *sanātana-dharma,* therefore, we must take it for granted on the authority of Śrīpāda Rāmānujācārya that it has neither beginning nor end. That which has neither end nor beginning must not be sectarian, for it cannot be limited by any boundaries. Those belonging to some sectarian faith will wrongly consider that *sanātana-dharma* is also sectarian, but if we go deeply into the matter and consider it in the light of modern science, it is possible for us to see that *sanātana dharma* is the business of all the people of the world—nay, of all the living entities of the universe."

"Non-*sanātana* religious faith may have some beginning in the annals of human history, but there is no beginning to the history of *sanātana-dharma,* because it remains eternally with the living entities. Insofar as the living entities are concerned, the authoritative *śāstras* state that the living entity has neither birth nor death. In the Gītā, it is stated that the living entity is never born and he never dies. He is eternal and indestructible, and he continues to live after the destruction of his temporary material body. In reference to the concept of *sanātana-dharma,* we must try to understand the concept of religion from the Sanskrit root meaning of the word. *Dharma* refers to that which constantly exists with a particular object. We conclude that there is heat and light along with the fire; without heat and light, there is no meaning to the word fire. Similarly, we must discover the essential part of the living being, that part which is his constant companion. That constant companion is his eternal quality, and that eternal quality is his eternal religion."

Lecture on BG 2.24 -- Hyderabad, November 28, 1972:

So there are so many questions that if we actually, philosophically study, then we can see vāsudevaḥ sarvam iti sa mahātmā sudurlabhaḥ (BG 7.19), how Vāsudeva, Kṛṣṇa is acting. Aṇḍāntara-stha-paramāṇu-cayāntara-stham (Bs. 5.35). So here the living entity is described as sanātana. And the process by which we can understand our sanātana nature, that is called sanātana-dharma, not that having a big tilaka and considering this rascal lump of matter as "I am brāhmaṇa. This body is brāhmaṇa, and sanātana-dharma." This is all nonsense. Sanātana-dharma means you first of all you must know what you are. That is sanātana-dharma. Is it... Is sanātana-dharma is limited to a certain area? How it can be? Sarva-gataḥ. Sanātana-dharma must be there everywhere. Īśāvāsyam idaṁ sarvam (ISO 1). Everywhere, Kṛṣṇa's kingdom, Kṛṣṇa's property. How is that you are simply claiming that "India, there is sanātana-dharma"? "In India there is brāhmaṇa"? What Kṛṣṇa creates, that is for everywhere. Because Kṛṣṇa is the father of everyone.

Dharma, if we take these two words... Sanātana means eternal. That is called sanātana. And dharma, dharma means occupation, characteristic. Dharma does not mean some superficial ritualistic ceremonies. Dharma means the characteristic. That is real meaning. Dharma is not a kind of faith. Dharma is characteristic. Sanātana-dharma means sanātana characteristic, eternal characteristic. The changing... Now, I have got now this body, Indian body, and then, next body may be cat's and dog's or demigod's, according to my karma. So the body changes. So sanātana-dharma cannot be applied to this body. Sanātana-dharma means the characteristic of the soul. That is sanātana-dharma, to understand the characteristic of the soul. Kṛṣṇa is describing here the characteristic of the soul: sanātana. And at the conclusion, He gives you information of the sanātana-dharma. What is that? Sarva-dharmān parityajya mām ekaṁ śaraṇaṁ vraja (BG 18.66). This is sanātana-dharma. Kṛṣṇa is sanātana, I am sanātana, you are sanātana.

So things are going on like... So sanātana-dharma means when one understands his real position, his real posi... that is self-realization. Or, in other words, Kṛṣṇa is sanātana. If you engage yourself in the service of Kṛṣṇa, then, by practicing the sanātana-dharma, you are transferred to the sanātana place, Vaikuṇṭha. That is sanātana-dharma. Dharma means characteristic. So what is our characteristic? I was going to explain. That we are now serving our senses. This is our material characteristic. Material characteristic because originally I am servant. I am not master. But I have given up service of Kṛṣṇa. Kṛṣṇa-bahirmukha hañā bhoga vāñchā kare (Prema-vivarta). "Why shall I become servant? I shall become Kṛṣṇa." All right, you become Kṛṣṇa. You become enjoyer. That is material world. Everyone is trying to become Kṛṣṇa, enjoyer. So there is fight. Always. You are becoming, trying to becoming Kṛṣṇa. I am trying to become Kṛṣṇa. As there are so many incarnations of God nowadays—every lane, every street.

Lecture on BG 2.25 -- Hyderabad, November 29, 1972:

So real our relationship with God, Kṛṣṇa, is to serve Him. Jīvera svarūpa haya nitya-kṛṣṇa-dāsa (Cc. Madhya 20.108-109). Anādi bahirmukha jīva kṛṣṇa bhuli gela, ataeva kṛṣṇa veda purāṇa kailā (CC Madhya 20.117). We have forgotten real position, sanātana-dharma. We have forgotten. Sanātana-dharma means a living entity is meant for serving the whole. Living entity's a part, part of the whole. So the living entity's business is to serve the whole. Just like this finger. This finger is the part of my body. Its business is to carry out my order, to serve the whole. I want the finger to come here. Immediately... Similarly, our business is to serve Kṛṣṇa, but when we want to become lord, independent of Kṛṣṇa, that is called māyā. Kṛṣṇa-bahirmukha hañā bhoga vāñchā kare, nikaṭa-stha māyā tāre jāpaṭiyā dhare. This is a statement in the Prema-vivarta. As soon as we desire to imitate Kṛṣṇa, that is māyā. Māyā is nothing. We create that situation of māyā. What is that? "I want to become Kṛṣṇa. I want to become God. I want to become the Lord." This is māyā. This is not possible. So Kṛṣṇa is sanātana. We are also sanātana. But when we forget to serve Kṛṣṇa, that is our asanātana. And when we are engaged again in the service of Kṛṣṇa, that is sanātana-dharma. So sanātana-dharma means eternally serving Kṛṣṇa. Another example, dharma... What is dharma? Dhṛ-dhātu. Characteristic. You cannot change it.

Lecture on BG 16.8 -- Hyderabad, December 16, 1976:

So the cultivation of knowledge how one can go back to that sanātana-dhāma and associate with the supreme sanātana and remain yourself sanātana, that is called sanātana-dharma. So we have to cultivate that sanātana-dharma, means we have to purify ourself from the material qualification or material designation. Here we have got material designation: "I am Indian," "I am American," "I am Hindu," "I am Muslim," "I am brāhmaṇa," "I am this and that." So one has to become free. That is purification, when we understand that, as Caitanya Mahāprabhu introduced Himself, that "I am not a brāhmaṇa, I am not a kṣatriya, I am not a śūdra, I am not a sannyāsī, I am not a brahmacārī, but I am servant of the servant of Kṛṣṇa (CC Madhya 13.80)." Gopī-bhartuḥ pada-kamalayor dāsa-dāsa-dāsānudāsaḥ. If we come to this understanding, that is our purification.

Lecture on SB 1.16.19 -- Hawaii, January 15, 1974:

Actually, Hindu is not a religion. Hindu is a name given by the foreigners. The religion is, of India, varṇāśrama-dharma, following the institution of four varṇas and four āśramas. That is varṇ... Or sanātana-dharma. Sanātana-dharma means eternal, eternal religion. Religion of human being is one. That is called sanātana. A living entity is described as sanātana. Mamaivāṁśo jīva-bhūto jīva-loke sanātanaḥ (BG 15.7). In the Bhagavad-gītā you'll find sanātanaḥ, and Kṛṣṇa is also addressed in the Eleventh Chapter as sanātanas tvam. And there is another place, or spiritual world, which is also called sanātana. In the Bhagavad-gītā you'll find, paras tasmāt tu bhāvo 'nyo 'vyakto 'vyaktāt sanātanaḥ (BG 8.20). So this sanātana term is very important. The living entity is sanātana and God is sanātana and the spiritual world is sanātana, and the process by which your lost relationship with God established and you go back to home back to Godhead, that is called sanātana-dharma. Sanātana-dharma. That is our eternal relationship with God.

. . .

Lecture on SB 6.2.12-14 -- Allahabad, January 17, 1971, at Kumbha-mela:

Actually, religion does not mean to improve your material condition. That is not religion. Śrīmad-Bhāgavata therefore says that sa vai puṁsāṁ paro dharmo yato bhaktir adhokṣaje: (SB 1.2.6) "That type of religion is first class which elevates one to the platform of pure devotional service to the Absolute Truth." That is religion. People are not attracted to the bhāgavata-dharma, or the religion. Bhāgavata-dharma is actually sanātana-dharma. Sanātana-dharma does not mean that one must have a certain type of religious life. Sanātana-dharma means the eternal religion. Sanātana-dharma is applicable for all living entities. A living entity is eternal, God is eternal, and there is an eternal abode also. Paras tasmāt tu bhāvo 'nyo 'vyakto 'vyaktāt sanātanaḥ (BG 8.20). So the religious principles which promote a follower to the highest platform of serving the eternal, supreme God, that is called sanātana-dharma. Nityo nityānāṁ cetanaś cetanānām (Kaṭha Upaniṣad 2.2.13). That is first-class religion.

Rotary Club Lecture -- Ahmedabad, December 5, 1972:

So the sanātana-dharma means that to find out the eternal engagement of the living entity. At the present moment, the living entity is changing the position. As we change our position even during this life—sometimes I am working in this office, sometimes working in that office, sometimes in this way, sometimes that way—similarly, we are changing eternally. We are creating our desires within the mind, thinking, feeling and willing, and according to the thinking, feeling and willing, we are getting a certain type of body, one after another. This is the process. Dehino 'smin yathā dehe kaumāraṁ yauvanaṁ jarā, tathā dehāntaraṁ prāptir (BG 2.13). Just like in this span of life, I was a child. Everyone was. Everyone remembers. Then I became a boy. I was playing. I can remember what I was doing in my childhood, boyhood. Then I became a young man. That also I remember. But those things have passed as dream. Now I am a different condition of life as old man. But I, the spirit soul, I remember that I was a child, I was a baby, I was a boy, I was a young man. Now I am old man. So the conclusion should be that although I have changed my bodies, I remember all these things. So the body and the remembering capacity, mean the subtle body, thinking, feeling and willing... That is called subtle body.

So the conclusion should be that sanātana-dharma means that the living entity is eternal, he must seek out his eternal service. That is called sanātana-dharma. Sanātana-dharma does not mean that having a great big tuft, and tilaka, or dressing in a certain manner, or... Then everything are changing. That is not sanātana-dharma. Whatever is changeable, that is not sanā-tana-dharma. Sanātana, try to understand sanātana. Sanātana means eternal, and the living entity, being eternal, he must have some eternal engagement. That is called sanātana-dharma

Srimad Bhagavatam

Canto 5 Chapter 19 Text 21

एतदेव हि देवा गायन्ति—
अहो अमीषां किमकारि शोभनं
प्रसन्न एषां स्विदुत स्वयं हरिः ।
यैर्जन्म लब्धं नृषु भारताजिरे
मुकुन्दसेवौपयिकं स्पृहा हि नः ॥ २१ ॥

etad eva hi deva gayanti
aho amisam kim akari sobhanam
prasanna esam svid uta svayam harih
yair janma labdham nrsu bharatajire
mukunda-sevaupayikam sprha hi nah

Translation

Since the human form of life is the sublime position for spiritual realization, all the demigods in heaven speak in this way: How wonderful it is for these human beings to

have been born in the land of Bhārata-varṣa. They must have executed pious acts of austerity in the past, or the Supreme Personality of Godhead Himself must have been pleased with them. Otherwise, how could they engage in devotional service in so many ways? We demigods can only aspire to achieve human births in Bhārata-varṣa to execute devotional service, but these human beings are already engaged there.

(Srimad Bhagavatam 5-19-21)

PURPORT

These facts are further explained in *Sri Caitanya-caritāmṛta* (*Ādi* 9.41):

bhārata-bhūmite haila manuṣya-janma yāra
janma sārthaka kari' kara para-upakāra

"One who has taken his birth as a human being in the land of India [Bhārata-varṣa] should make his life successful and work for the benefit of all other people."

There are many facilities in India, Bhārata-varṣa, for executing devotional service. In Bhārata-varṣa, all the *ācāryas* contributed their experience, and Śrī Caitanya Mahāprabhu personally appeared to teach the people of Bhārata-varṣa how to progress in spiritual life and be fixed in devotional service to the Lord. From all points of view, Bhārata-varṣa is the special land where one can very easily understand the process of devotional service and adopt it to make his life successful. If one makes his life successful in devotional service and then preaches devotional service in other parts of the world, people throughout the world will actually benefit.

Srimad Bhagavatam

किं दुष्करैर्नः क्रतुभिस्तपोव्रतै-
र्दानादिभिर्वा द्युजयेन फल्गुना ।
न यत्र नारायणपादपङ्कज-
स्मृतिः प्रमुष्टातिशयेन्द्रियोत्सवात् ॥ २२ ॥

*kiṁ duṣkarair naḥ kratubhis tapo-vratair
dānādibhir vā dyujayena phalgunā
na yatra narayaṇa-pāda-paṅkaja-
smṛtiḥ pramuṣṭātiśayendriyotsavāt*

Translation

The demigods continue: After performing the very difficult tasks of executing Vedic ritualistic sacrifices, undergoing austerities, observing vows and giving charity, we have achieved this position as inhabitants of the heavenly planets. But what is the value of this achievement? Here we are certainly very engaged in material

sense gratification, and therefore we can hardly remember the lotus feet of Lord Nārāyaṇa. Indeed, because of our excessive sense gratification, we have almost forgotten His lotus feet.

(Srimad Bhagavatam 5-19-22)

PURPORT

The land of Bhārata-varṣa is so exalted that by taking birth there, one can not only attain the heavenly planets but also go directly back home, back to Godhead. As Kṛṣṇa says in *Bhagavad-gītā* (9.25):

$$yānti \ deva\text{-}vratā \ devān$$
$$pitṝn \ yānti \ pitṛ\text{-}vratāḥ$$
$$bhūtāni \ yānti \ bhūtejyā$$
$$yānti \ mad\text{-}yājino \ 'pi \ mām$$

"Those who worship the demigods will take birth among the demigods; those who worship ghosts and spirits will take birth among such beings; those who worship ancestors go to the ancestors; and those who worship Me will live with Me."

People in the land of Bhārata-varṣa generally follow the Vedic principles and consequently perform great sacrifices by which they can be elevated to the heavenly planets. However, what is the use of such great attainments? As stated in *Bhagavad-gītā* (9.21), *kṣīṇe puṇye martya-lokaṁ viśanti:* after the results of one's sacrifices, charity and other pious activities expire, one must return to the lower planetary systems and again feel the pangs of birth and death. However, one who becomes Kṛṣṇa conscious can go back to Kṛṣṇa (*yānti-mad-yājino 'pi mām*). Therefore, the demigods even regret having been elevated to the higher planetary systems. The denizens of the heavenly planets regret that they could not take full advantage of being born in the land of Bhārata-varṣa. Instead, they became captivated by a higher standard of sense gratification, and therefore they forgot the lotus feet of Lord Nārāyaṇa at the time of death. The conclusion is that one who has taken birth in the land of Bhārata-varṣa must follow the instructions given personally by the Supreme Personality of Godhead. *Yad gatvā na nivartante tad dhāma paramaṁ mama.* One should try to return home, back to Godhead, to the Vaikuṇṭha planets — or to the topmost Vaikuṇṭha planet, Goloka Vṛndāvana — to live eternally in full, blissful knowledge in the company of the Supreme Personality of Godhead.

Srimad Bhagavatam

Canto 5 Chapter 19 Text 23

कल्पायुषां स्थानजयात्पुनर्भवात्
क्षणायुषां भारतभूजयो वरम् ।
क्षणेन मर्त्येन कृतं मनस्विनः
सन्न्यस्य संयान्त्यभयं पदं हरेः ॥ २३ ॥

kalpāyuṣāṁ sthānajayāt punar-bhavāt
kṣaṇāyuṣāṁ bhārata-bhūjayo varam
kṣaṇena martyena kṛtaṁ manasvinaḥ
sannyasya saṁyānty abhayaṁ padaṁ harcḥ

Translation

A short life in the land of Bharata-varṣa is preferable to a life achieved in Brahmaloka for millions and billions of years because even if one is elevated to Brahmaloka, he must return to repeated birth and death. Although life in Bhārata-varṣa, in a lower planetary system, is very

short, one who lives there can elevate himself to full Kṛṣṇa consciousness and achieve the highest perfection, even in this short life, by fully surrendering unto the lotus feet of the Lord. Thus, one attains Vaikuṇṭhaloka, where there is neither anxiety nor repeated birth in a material body.

(*Srimad Bhagavatam* 5.19.23)

PURPORT

This is further confirmation of the statement given by Lord Caitanya Mahāprabhu:

bhārata-bhūmite haila manuṣya-janma yāra
janma sārthaka kari' kara para-upakāra

One who has taken birth in the land of Bhārata-varṣa has a full opportunity to study the direct instructions given by Kṛṣṇa in *Bhagavad-gītā* and thus finally decide what to do in his human form of life. One should certainly give up all other propositions and surrender to Kṛṣṇa. Kṛṣṇa will then immediately take charge and relieve one of the results of past sinful life (*ahaṁ tvāṁ sarva-pāpebhyo mokṣayiṣyāmi mā śucaḥ*). Therefore, one should take to Kṛṣṇa consciousness, as Kṛṣṇa Himself recommends. *Man-manā bhava mad-bhakto mad-yājī māṁ namaskuru:* "Always think of Me, become My devotee, worship Me and offer Me obeisances." This is very easy, even for a child. Why not take this path? One should try to follow the instructions of Kṛṣṇa exactly and thus become fully eligible to be promoted to the kingdom of God (*tyaktvā deham punar janma naiti mām eti so 'rjuna*). One should go directly to Kṛṣṇa and engage in His service. This is the best opportunity offered to the inhabitants of Bhārata-varṣa. One who is fit to return home, back to Godhead, is no longer liable to the results of *karma,* good or bad.

Srimad Bhagavatam

प्राप्ता नृजातिं त्विह ये च जन्तवो
ज्ञानक्रियाद्रव्यकलापसम्भृताम् ।
न वै यतेरन्नपुनर्भवाय ते
भूयो वनौका इव यान्ति बन्धनम् ॥ २५ ॥

prāptā nṛ-jātiṁ tv iha ye ca jantavo
jñāna-kriyā-dravya-kalāpa-sambhṛtām
na vai yaterann apunar-bhavāya tc
bhūyo vanaukā iva yānti bandhanam

Translation

Bhārata-varṣa offers the proper land and circumstances in which to execute devotional service, which can free one from the results of jñāna and karma. If one obtains a human body in the land of Bhārata-varṣa, with clear sensory organs with which to execute the saṅkīrtana-yajña, but in spite of this opportunity he does not take

to devotional service, he is certainly like liberated forest animals and birds that are careless and are therefore again bound by a hunter.

(Srimad Bhagavatam 5.19.25)

PURPORT

In the land of Bhārata-varṣa one can very easily perform the *saṅkīrtana-yajña,* which consists of *śravaṇaṁ kīrtanaṁ viṣṇoḥ,* or one can perform other methods of devotional service, such as *smaraṇaṁ vandanaṁ arcanaṁ dāsyaṁ sakhyam* and *ātma-nivedanam.* In Bhārata-varṣa one has the opportunity to visit many holy places, especially Lord Caitanya's birthsite and Lord Kṛṣṇa's birthsite — Navadvīpa and Vṛndāvana — where there are many pure devotees who have no desire other than to execute devotional service (*anyāb-hilāṣitā-śūnyaṁ jñāna-karmādy-anāvṛtam*), and one may thus become free from the bondage of material conditions. Other paths, such as the path of *jñāna* and the path of *karma,* are not very profitable. Pious activities can elevate one to the higher planetary systems, and by speculative knowl-edge one can merge into the Brahman existence, but that is not real profit, for one has to come down again even from the liberated condition of being merged in Brahman, and certainly one must come down from the heavenly kingdom. One should endeavor to go back home, back to Godhead (*yānti mad-yājino 'pi mām*). Otherwise, there is no difference between human life and the lives of jungle animals and birds. Animals and birds also have freedom, but because of their lower birth, they cannot use it. Taking advantage of all the facilities offered him, a human being who has taken birth in the land of Bhārata-varṣa should become a fully enlightened devotee and go back home, back to Godhead. This is the subject matter of the Kṛṣṇa consciousness movement. The inhabitants of places other than Bhārata-varṣa have facilities for material enjoyment, but they do not have the same facility to take to Kṛṣṇa consciousness. Therefore, Śrī Caitanya Mahāprabhu has advised that one who has taken birth as a human being in Bhārata-varṣa must first realize himself as part and parcel of Kṛṣṇa, and after taking to Kṛṣṇa consciousness, he must distribute this knowledge all over the world.

यद्यत्र नः स्वर्गसुखावशेषितं
स्विष्टस्य सूक्तस्य कृतस्य शोभनम् ।
तेनाजनाभे स्मृतिमज्जन्म नः स्याद्
वर्षे हरिर्यद्द्रजतां शं तनोति ॥ २८ ॥

yady atra naḥ svarga-sukhāvaśeṣitaṁ
sviṣṭasya sūktasya kṛtasya śobhanam
tenājanābhe smṛtimaj janma naḥ syād
varṣe harir yad-bhajatāṁ śaṁ tanoti

TRANSLATION

We are now living on the heavenly planets, undoubtedly as a result of our having performed ritualistic ceremonies, pious activities and yajñas and having studied the Vedas. However, our lives here will one day be finished. We pray that at that time, if any merit remains from our pious activities, we may again take birth in

Bhārata-varṣa as human beings able to remember the lotus feet of the Lord. The Lord is so kind that He personally comes to the land of Bhārata-varṣa and expands the good fortune of its people.

(*Srimad Bhagavatam* 5.19.28)

PURPORT

It is certainly as a result of pious activities that one takes birth in the heavenly planets, but from those planets one must nevertheless come down again to earth, as stated in *Bhagavad-gītā* (*kṣīṇe puṇye martya-lokaṁ viśanti*). Even the demigods must return to earth to work like ordinary men when the results of their pious activities expire. Nevertheless, the demigods desire to come to the land of Bhārata-varṣa if even a small portion of the merits of their pious activities remains. In other words, to take birth in Bhārata-varṣa, one must perform more pious activities than the demigods. In Bhārata-varṣa one is naturally Kṛṣṇa conscious, and if one further cultivates his Kṛṣṇa consciousness, by the grace of Kṛṣṇa he certainly expands his good fortune by becoming perfect in Kṛṣṇa consciousness and very easily going back home, back to Godhead. In many other places in the Vedic literature, it is found that even the demigods want to come to this land of Bhārata-varṣa. A foolish person may desire to be promoted to the heavenly planets as a result of his pious activities, but even the demigods from the heavenly planets want to come to Bhārata-varṣa and achieve bodies that may be very easily used to cultivate Kṛṣṇa consciousness. Therefore, Śrī Caitanya Mahāprabhu repeatedly says:

bhārata-bhūmite haila manuṣya-janma yāra
janma sārthaka kari' kara para-upakāra

A human being born in the land of Bhārata-varṣa has the special prerogative to develop Kṛṣṇa consciousness. Therefore, those already born in Bhārata-varṣa should take lessons from the *śāstras* and *guru* and should fully take advantage of the mercy of Śrī Caitanya Mahāprabhu in order to be fully equipped with Kṛṣṇa consciousness. By taking full advantage of Kṛṣṇa consciousness, one goes back home, back to Godhead (*yānti mad-yājino 'pi mām*). The Kṛṣṇa consciousness movement is therefore spreading this facility to human society by opening many, many centers all over the world so that people may associate with the pure devotees of the Kṛṣṇa consciousness movement, understand the science of Kṛṣṇa consciousness and ultimately go back home, back to Godhead.

Srimad Bhagavatam

Canto 5 Chapter 19 Text 19

अस्मिन्नेव वर्षे पुरुषैर्लब्ध्यजन्मभि: शुक्ललोहितकृष्णवर्णेन स्वारब्धेन
कर्मणा दिव्यमानुषनारकगतयो बह्व्य: आत्मन आनुपूर्व्येण सर्वा ह्येव
सर्वेषां विधीयन्ते यथावर्णविधानमपवर्गश्चापि भवति ॥ १९ ॥

*asminn eva varṣe puruṣair labdha-janmabhiḥ śukla-lohita-
kṛṣṇa-varṇena svārabdhena karmaṇā divya-mānuṣa-nāraka-
gatayo bahvya ātmana ānupūrvyeṇa sarvā hy eva sarveṣāṁ
vidhīyante yathā-varṇa-vidhānam upavargaś cāpi bhavati*

TRANSLATION

The people who take birth in this tract of land are
divided according to the qualities of material nature —
the modes of goodness [sattva-guṇa], passion [rajo-
guṇa], and ignorance [tamo-guṇa]. Some of them are
born as exalted personalities, some are ordinary human
beings, and some are extremely abominable, for in
Bhārata-varṣa one takes birth exactly according to one's

past karma. **If one's position is ascertained by a bona fide spiritual master and one is properly trained to engage in the service of Lord Viṣṇu according to the four social divisions [brāhmaṇa, kṣatriya, vaiśya and śūdra] and the four spiritual divisions [brahmacārī, gṛhastha, vānaprastha and sannyāsa], one's life becomes perfect.**

(Srimad Bhagavatam 5.19.19)

PURPORT

For further information, one should refer to *Bhagavad-gītā* (14.18 and 18.42-45). Śrīla Rāmānujācārya writes in his book *Vedārtha-saṅgraha:*

evaṁ-vidha-parābhakti-svarūpa-jñāna-viśeṣasyotpādakaḥ pūrvoktāharahar   upacīyamāna-jñāna-pūrvaka-karmānugṛhīta-bhakti-yoga   eva; yathoktaṁ   bhagavatā parāśareṇa — varṇāśrameti. nikhila-jagad-uddhāraṇāyāvani-tale 'vatīrṇaṁ para-brahma-bhūtaḥ puruṣottamaḥ svayam etad uktavān — "svakarma-nirataḥ siddhiṁ yathā vindati tac chṛṇu" "yataḥ pravṛttir bhūtānāṁ yena sarvam idaṁ tatam/ svakarmaṇā tam abhyarcya siddhiṁ vindati mānavaḥ."

In the *Viṣṇu Purāṇa* (3.8.9), the great sage Parāśara Muni has recommended:

varṇāśramācāravatā
puruṣeṇa paraḥ pumān
viṣṇur ārādhyate panthā
nānyat tat-toṣa-kāraṇam

"The Supreme Personality of Godhead, Lord Viṣṇu, is worshiped by the proper execution of prescribed duties in the system of *varṇa* and *āśrama*. There is no other way to satisfy the Lord." In the land of Bhārata-varṣa, the institution of *varṇāśrama-dharma* may be easily adopted. At the present moment, certain demoniac sections of the population of Bhārata-varṣa are disregarding the system of *varṇāśrama-dharma*. Because there is no institution to teach people how to become *brāhmaṇas, kṣatriyas, vaiśyas* and *śūdras* or *brahmacārīs, gṛhasthas, vānaprasthas* and *sannyāsīs,* these demons want a classless society. This results in chaotic conditions. In the name of secular government, unqualified people are taking the supreme governmental posts. No one is being trained to act according to the principles of *varṇāśrama-dharma,* and thus people are becoming increasingly degraded and are heading in the direction of animal life. The real aim of life is liberation, but unfortunately, the opportunity for liberation is being denied to people in general, and therefore their human lives are being spoiled. The Kṛṣṇa consciousness movement, however, is being propagated all over the world to reestablish the *varṇāśrama-dharma* system and thus save human society from gliding down to hellish life.

Srimad Bhagavatam

Canto 6 Chapter 16 Text 58

लब्ध्वेह मानुषीं योनिं ज्ञानविज्ञानसम्भवाम् ।
आत्मानं यो न बुद्ध्येत न क्वचित्क्षेममाप्नुयात् ॥ ५८ ॥

*labdhveha mānuṣīṁ yoniṁ jñāna-vijñāna-sambhavām
ātmānaṁ yo na buddhyeta na kvacit kṣemam āpnuyāt*

Translation

A human being can attain perfection in life by self-realization through the Vedic literature and its practical application. This is possible especially for a human being born in India, the land of piety. A man who obtains birth in such a convenient position but does not understand his self is unable to achieve the highest perfection, even if he is exalted to life in the higher planetary systems.

(*Srimad Bhagavatam* 6.16.58)

Purport

This statement is confirmed in *Caitanya-caritāmṛta* (*Ādi* 9.41). Lord Caitanya said:

bhārata-bhūmite haila manuṣya-janma yāra
janma sārthaka kari' kara para-upakāra

Everyone born in India, especially as a human being, can achieve the supreme success through the Vedic literature and its practical application in life. When one is perfect, he can render a service for the self-realization of the entire human society. This is the best way to perform humanitarian work.

Srimad Bhagavatam

न यत्र वैकुण्ठकथासुधापगा
न साधवो भागवतास्तदाश्रया: ।
न यत्र यज्ञेशमखा महोत्सवा:
सुरेशलोकोऽपि न वै स सेव्यताम् ॥ २४ ॥

*na yatra vaikuntha-katha-sudhapaga na sadhavo bhagavatas
tadasrayah
na yatra yajnesa-makha mahotsavah suresa-loko 'pi na vai sa
sevyatam*

Translation

An intelligent person does not take an interest in a place,
even in the topmost planetary system, if the pure Ganges
of topics concerning the Supreme Lord's activities does
not flow there, if there are no devotees engaged in service
on the banks of such a river of piety, or if there are no

festivals of saṅkīrtana-yajña to satisfy the Lord [especially since saṅkīrtana-yajña is recommended in this age].

(*Srimad Bhagavatam*-5.19.24)

Purport

Śrī Caitanya Mahāprabhu appeared in the land of Bhārata-varṣa, specifically in Bengal, in the district of Nadia, where Navadvīpa is situated. It is, therefore, to be concluded, as stated by Śrīla Bhaktivinoda Ṭhākura, that within this universe, this earth is the best planet, and on this planet the land of Bhārata-varṣa is the best; in the land of Bhārata-varṣa, Bengal is still better, in Bengal the district of Nadia is still better, and in Nadia, the best place is Navadvīpa because Śrī Caitanya Mahāprabhu appeared there to inaugurate the performance of the sacrifice of chanting the Hare Kṛṣṇa *mahā-mantra*. The *śāstras* recommend:

> *kṛṣṇa-varṇaṁ tviṣākṛṣṇaṁ*
> *sāṅgopāṅgāstra-pārṣadam*
> *yajñaiḥ saṅkīrtana-prāyair*
> *yajanti hi sumedhasaḥ*

Lord Śrī Caitanya Mahāprabhu is always accompanied by His very confidential associates such as Śrī Nityānanda, Śrī Gadādhara and Śrī Advaita and by many devotees like Śrīvāsa. They are always engaged in chanting the name of the Lord and are always describing Lord Kṛṣṇa. Therefore, this is the best among all the places in the universe. The Kṛṣṇa consciousness movement has established its center in Māyāpur, the birthsite of Lord Śrī Caitanya Mahāprabhu, to give men the great opportunity to go there and perform a constant festival of *saṅkīrtana-yajña,* as recommended herein (*yajñeśa-makhā mahotsavāḥ*) and to distribute *prasāda* to millions of hungry people hankering for spiritual emancipation. This is the mission of the Kṛṣṇa consciousness movement. *Caitanya-bhāgavata* confirms this as follows: "One should not desire to be elevated even to a place in the heavenly planetary systems if it has no propaganda to expand the glories of the Supreme Personality of Godhead, no trace of Vaiṣṇavas, pure devotees of the Lord, and no festivals for spreading Kṛṣṇa consciousness. It would be better to live perpetually cramped within the airtight bag of a mother's womb, where one can at least remember the lotus feet of the Lord, than to live in a place where there is no opportunity to remember His lotus feet. I pray not to be allowed to take birth in such a condemned place."

Similarly, in *Caitanya-caritāmṛta,* Kṛṣṇadāsa Kavirāja Gosvāmī says that since Śrī Caitanya Mahāprabhu is the inaugurator of the *saṅkīrtana* movement, anyone who performs *saṅkīrtana* to please the Lord is very, very glorious. Such a person has perfect intelligence, whereas others are in ignorance of material existence. Of all the sacrifices mentioned in the Vedic literature, the performance of *saṅkīrtana-yajña* is the best. Even the performance of one hundred *aśvamedha* sacrifices cannot compare to the sacrifice of *saṅkīrtana.* According to the author of *Śrī Caitanya-caritāmṛta,* if one compares *saṅkīrtana-yajña* to other *yajñas,* he is a *pāṣaṇḍī,* an infidel, and is liable to be punished by Yamarāja. There are many Māyāvādīs who think that the performance of *saṅkīrtana-yajña* is a pious activity similar to the performance of the *aśvamedha-yajña* and other such pious functions, but this is a *nāma-aparādha*. Chanting of the holy name of Nārāyaṇa and chanting of other names are never equal, despite what Māyāvādīs think.

Sri Chaitanya Charitamrta

Here are further explanations of this famous verse quoted so many times by Srila Prabhupada from the Sri Caitanya Caritamrta (Madhya-lila 25.264)...

> *bhārata-bhūmite haila manuṣya-janma yāra*
> *janma sārthaka kari' kara para-upakāra*

...making the point and case for all human's beings born in Bharata-varsha to take up the direct order of Lord Sri Caitanya Mahaprabhu

The magnanimity of Lord Caitanya Mahāprabhu is expressed in this very important verse. Although He was born in Bengal and Bengalis, therefore, have a special duty toward Him, Śrī Caitanya Mahāprabhu is addressing not only Bengalis but all the inhabitants of India. It is in the land of India that actual human civilization can be developed.

Human life is especially meant for God realization, as stated in the *Vedānta-sūtra: athāto brahma-jijñāsā*. Anyone who takes birth in the land of India (Bhārata-varṣa) has the special privilege of being able to take advantage of the instruction and guidance of the Vedic civilization. He automatically receives the basic principles of spiritual life, for 99.9% of the Indian people, even simple village farmers and others who are neither educated nor sophisticated, believe in the transmigration of the soul, believe in past and future lives, believe in God and naturally want to worship the Supreme Personality of Godhead or His representative. These ideas are the natural inheritance of a person born in India. India has many holy places of pilgrimage, such as Gayā, Benares, Mathurā, Prayāga, Vṛndāvana, Haridvāra, Rāmeśvaram and Jagannātha Purī, and still people go there by the hundreds and thousands.

Although the present leaders of India are influencing the people not to believe in God, not to believe in the next life and not to believe in a distinction between pious and impious life, and they are teaching them how to drink wine, eat meat and become supposedly civilized, people are nevertheless afraid of the four activities of sinful life-namely, illicit sex, meat-eating, intoxication and gambling-and whenever there is a religious festival, they gather together by the thousands.

We have actual experience of this. Whenever the Kṛṣṇa consciousness movement holds a *saṅkīrtana* festival in a big city like Calcutta, Bombay, Madras, Ahmedabad, or Hyderabad, thousands of people come to hear. Sometimes we speak in English, but even though most people do not understand English, they nevertheless come to hear us. Even when imitation incarnations of Godhead speak, people gather in the thousands, for everyone who is born in the land of India has a natural spiritual inclination and is taught the basic principles of spiritual life; they merely need to be a little more educated in the Vedic principles. Therefore Śrī Caitanya Mahāprabhu said, *janma sārthaka kari' kara para-upakāra:* if an Indian is educated in the Vedic principles, he is able to perform the most beneficial welfare activity for the entire world.

At present, for want of Kṛṣṇa consciousness, or God-consciousness, the entire world is in darkness, having been covered by the four principles of sinful life-meat-eating, illicit sex, gambling and intoxication. Therefore, there is a need for vigorous propaganda to educate people to refrain from sinful activities. This will bring peace and prosperity; the rogues, thieves and debauchees will naturally decrease in number, and all of human society will be God-conscious.

The practical effect of our spreading the Kṛṣṇa consciousness movement all over the world is that now the most degraded debauchees are becoming the most elevated saints. This is only one Indian's humble service to the world. If all Indians had taken to this path, as advised by Lord Caitanya Mahāprabhu, India would have given a unique gift to the world, and thus India would have been glorified.

Now, however, India is known as a poverty-stricken country, and whenever anyone from America or another opulent country goes to India, he sees many people lying by the foot-paths for whom there are not even provisions for two meals a day. There are also institutions collecting money from all parts of the world in the name of welfare activities for poverty-stricken people, but they are spending it for their own sense gratification. Now, on the order of Śrī Caitanya Mahāprabhu, the Kṛṣṇa consciousness movement has been started, and people are benefiting from this movement.

Therefore, it is now the duty of the leading men of India to consider the importance of this movement and train many Indians to go outside of India to preach this cult. People will accept it, there will be cooperation among the Indian people and among the other people of the world, and the mission of Śrī Caitanya Mahāprabhu will then be fulfilled.

Śrī Caitanya Mahāprabhu will then be glorified all over the world, and people will naturally be happy, peaceful and prosperous, not only in this life but also in the next, for as stated in the *Bhagavad-gītā,* anyone who understands Kṛṣṇa, the Supreme Personality of Godhead, will very easily get salvation, or freedom from the repetition of birth and death, and go back home, back to Godhead. Śrī Caitanya Mahāprabhu , therefore, requests every Indian to become a preacher of His cult to save the world from disastrous confusion.

This is not only the duty of Indians but the duty of everyone, and we are very happy that American and European boys and girls are seriously cooperating with this movement. One should know definitely that the best welfare activity for all of human society is to awaken man's God-consciousness or Kṛṣṇa consciousness. Therefore, everyone should help this great movement. This is confirmed in *Śrīmad-Bhāgavatam,* Tenth Canto, Twenty-second Chapter, verse 35, which is next quoted in *Caitanya-caritāmṛta.*

Text 42

एतावज्जन्मसाफल्यं देहिनामिह देहिषु ।
प्राणैरर्थैर्धिया वाचा श्रेयआचरणं सदा ॥ ३५ ॥

etāvaj janma-sāphalyaṁ dehinām iha dehiṣu
prāṇair arthair dhiyā vācā śreya-ācaraṇaṁ sadā

Translation

"It is the duty of every living being to perform welfare activities for the benefit of others with his life, wealth, intelligence and words."

Purport

There are two kinds of general activities-*śreyas,* or activities which are ultimately beneficial and auspicious, and *preyas,* or those which are immediately beneficial and auspicious. For example, children are fond of playing. They don't want to go to school to receive an education, and they think that playing all day and night and enjoy with their friends is the aim of life. Even in the transcendental life of Lord Kṛṣṇa, we find that when He was a child, He was very fond of playing with His friends of the same age, the cowherd boys. He would not even go home to take His dinner. Mother Yaśodā would have to come out to induce Him to come home. Thus, it is a child's nature to engage all day and night in playing, not caring even for his health and other important concerns. This is an example of *preyas,* or immediately beneficial activities. But there are also *śreyas,* or activities which are ultimately auspicious. According to Vedic civilization, a human being must be God-conscious. He should understand what God is, what this material world is, who he is, and what their interrelationships are. This is called *śreyas,* or ultimately auspicious activity.

In this verse of *Śrīmad-Bhāgavatam* it is said that one should be interested in *śreyas.* To achieve the ultimate goal of *śreyas,* or good fortune, one should engage everything, including his life, wealth and words, not only for himself but for others also. However, unless one is interested in *śreyas* in his own life, he cannot preach of *śreyas* for the benefit of others.

This verse cited by Śrī Caitanya Mahāprabhu applies to human beings, not to animals. As indicated in the previous verse by the words *manuṣya-janma,* these injunctions are for human beings. Unfortunately, human beings, although they have the bodies of men, are becoming less than animals in their behavior. This is the fault of modern education. Modern educators do not know the aim of human life; they are simply concerned with how to develop the economic condition of their countries or of human society. This is also necessary; the Vedic civilization considers all aspects of human life, including *dharma* (religion), *artha* (economic development), *kāma* (sense gratification) and *mokṣa* (liberation). But humanity's first concern should be religion. To be religious, one must abide by the orders of God, but unfortunately, people in this age have rejected religion, and they are busy in economic development. Therefore, they will adopt any means to get money. For economic development one does not need to get money by hook or by crook; one needs only sufficient money to maintain his body and soul. However, because modern economic development is going on with no religious background, people have become lusty, greedy and mad after money. They are simply developing the qualities of *rajas* (passion) and *tamas* (ignorance), neglecting the other quality of nature, *sattva* (goodness), and the brahminical qualifications. Therefore, the entire society is in chaos.

The *Bhāgavatam* says that it is the duty of an advanced human being to act in such a way as to facilitate human society's attainment of the ultimate goal of life. There is a similar verse in the *Viṣṇu Purāṇa,* Part Three, Chapter Twelve, verse 45, which is quoted in this chapter of *Caitanya-caritāmṛta* as verse 43.

Text 43

প্রাণিনামুপকারায় যদেবেহ পরত্র চ ।
কর্মণা মনসা বাচা তদেব মতিমান্ ভজেৎ ॥ ৪৩ ॥

prāṇinām upakārāya yad eveha paratra ca
karmaṇā manasā vācā tad eva mati-mān bhajet

TRANSLATION

Through his work, thoughts and words, an intelligent man must perform actions that will be beneficial for all living entities in this life and in the next.

Purport

Unfortunately, people, in general, do not know what is to take place in the next life. To prepare oneself for his next life is common sense, and it is a principle of the Vedic civilization, but presently people throughout the world do not believe in the next life. Even influential professors and other educators say that as soon as the body is finished, everything is finished. This atheistic philosophy is killing human civilization. People are irresponsibly performing all sorts of sinful activities, and thus the privilege of human life is being taken away by the educational propaganda of the so-called leaders. Actually, it is a fact that this life is meant for preparation for the next life; by evolution one has come through many species or forms, and this human form of life is an opportunity to promote oneself to a better life. This is explained in the *Bhagavad-gītā* (9.25):

> *yānti deva-vratā devān*
> *pitṛn yānti pitṛ-vratāḥ*
> *bhūtāni yānti bhūtejyā*
> *yānti mad-yājino 'pi mām*

"Those who worship the demigods will take birth among the demigods; those who worship ghosts and spirits will take birth among such beings; those who worship ancestors go to the ancestors; and those who worship Me will live with Me." Therefore, one may promote himself to the higher planetary systems, which are the residence of the demigods, one can promote himself to the Pitṛloka, one can remain on earth, or one can also go back home, back to Godhead. This is further confirmed elsewhere in the *Bhagavad-gītā* (4.9): *tyaktvā de-*

ham punar janma naiti mām eti so 'rjuna. After giving up the body, one who knows Kṛṣṇa in truth does not come back again to this world to accept a material body, but he goes back home, back to Godhead. This knowledge is in the *śāstras,* and people should be given the opportunity to understand it. Even if one is not able to go back to Godhead in one life, the Vedic civilization at least gives one the opportunity to be promoted to the higher planetary systems, where the demigods live and not glide down again to animal life. At present, people do not understand this knowledge, although it constitutes a great science, for they are uneducated and trained not to accept it. This is the horrible condition of modern human society. As such, the Kṛṣṇa consciousness movement is the only hope to direct the attention of intelligent men to a greater benefit in life.

bhārata-bhūmite haila manuṣya-janma yāra
janma sārthaka kari' kara para-upakāra

"All Indians should seriously take up the cult of Śrī Caitanya Mahāprabhu and should perfect their lives by adopting the process of devotional service. After perfecting their lives, they should broadcast this message all over the world for the welfare of all human beings [*para-upakāra*]." (Cc. *Ādi* 9.41) A Vaiṣṇava is especially interested in *para-upakāra,* doing good to others. Prahlāda Mahārāja was also interested in this. He did not want to be delivered alone; rather, he wanted to deliver all fallen souls, who are bereft of knowledge of *bhakti* and who misuse their intelligence for the temporary benefit of the material body. Śrī Caitanya Mahāprabhu also wanted His mission spread all over the world.

> *pṛthivīte āche yata nagarādi grāma*
> *sarvatra pracāra haibe mora nāma*

"In every town and village, the chanting of My name will be heard." (*Caitanya-bhāgavata, Antya* 4.126)

Following in the footsteps of Śrī Caitanya Mahāprabhu, we are trying to broadcast His message throughout the world. By His mercy, people are taking this movement very seriously. Indeed, our books are extensively distributed in Western countries, especially in America and Europe. Even the ecclesiastical orders in these countries appreciate the value of the Kṛṣṇa consciousness movement and are ready to unite for the highest benefit of human society. The followers of Śrī Caitanya Mahāprabhu may therefore take this movement seriously and broadcast it throughout the world, from village to village and from town to town, just as Śrī Caitanya Mahāprabhu Himself did.

In this Age of Kali, people are gradually becoming less than animals. Nevertheless, although they are eating the flesh of cows and are envious of brahminical culture, Śrī Caitanya Mahāprabhu is considering how to deliver them from this horrible condition of life. Thus, He asks all Indians to take up His mission (CC Antya-lila 3.51):

> *bhārata-bhūmite haila manuṣya-janma yāra*
> *janma sārthaka kari' kara para-upakāra*

"One who has taken his birth as a human being in the land of India [Bhārata-varṣa] should make his life successful and work for the benefit of all other people." (Cc. *Ādi-līlā* 9.41). It is, therefore, the duty of every advanced and cultured Indian to take this cause very seriously. All Indians should help the Kṛṣṇa consciousness movement in its progress to the best of their ability. Then they will be considered real followers of Śrī Caitanya Mahāprabhu. Unfortunately, even some so-called Vaiṣṇavas enviously refuse to cooperate with this movement but instead condemn it in so many ways. We are very sorry to say that these people are trying to find fault with us, being unnecessarily envious of our activities, although we are trying to the best of our ability to introduce the Kṛṣṇa consciousness movement directly into the countries of the *yavanas* and *mlecchas*. Such *yavanas* and *mlecchas* are coming to us and becoming purified Vaiṣṇavas who follow in the footsteps of Śrī Caitanya Mahāprabhu. One who identifies himself as a follower of Śrī Caitanya Mahāprabhu should feel like Śrī Caitanya Mahāprabhu, who said, *ihā-sabāra kon mate ha-ibe nistāra:* "How will all these *yavanas* be delivered?" Śrī Caitanya Mahāprabhu was always anxious to deliver the fallen souls because their fallen condition gave Him great unhappiness. That is the platform on which one can propagate the mission of Śrī Caitanya Mahāprabhu.

> *bhārata-bhūmite haila manuṣya-janma yāra*
> *janma sārthaka kari' kara para-upakāra*

One who has taken birth in the land of Bhārata-bhūmi, India, should take full advantage of his birth. He should become completely well-versed in the knowledge of the Vedas and spiritual culture and should distribute the experience of Kṛṣṇa consciousness all over the world. People all over the world are madly engaging in sense gratification and in this way spoiling their human lives, with the risk that in the next life they may become animals or less. Human society should be saved from such a risky civilization and the danger of animalism by awakening to God-consciousness, Kṛṣṇa consciousness. The Kṛṣṇa consciousness movement has been started for this purpose. Therefore, unbiased men of the highest echelon should study the principles of the Kṛṣṇa consciousness movement and fully cooperate with this movement to save human society.

ROOM CONVERSATION, MORNING WALKS ETC.

Now we share further explanations from Srila Prabhupada's lectures, conversations and morning walks where He specifically instructs all those who have taken birth in (Bharata-Varsha) India.

- CONVERSATION WITH LT. DAVID MOZEE CHICAGO POLICE DEPT. JULY 1975

Lieutenant Mozee: With all due respect, isn't it true that in India, where religious customs have been followed for centuries upon centuries, we are seeing not a return to but a drawing away from spiritual life?

Śrīla Prabhupāda: Yes, but it is due only to bad leadership. Otherwise, the vast majority of the Indian people are fully conscious of God, and they try to follow the laws of God. Here in the West, even big college professors do not believe in God or in life after death. But in India, even the poorest man believes in God and in a next life. He knows that if he commits sins he will suffer and if he acts piously, he will enjoy. To this day, if there is a disagreement between two villagers, they will go to the temple to settle it, because everyone knows that the opposite parties will hesitate to speak lies before the Deities. So, in most respects, India is still eighty percent religious. That is the special privilege of taking birth in India, and the special responsibility also. Śrī Caitanya Mahāprabhu has said:

> *bhārata-bhūmite haila manuṣya-janma yāra*
> *janma sārthaka kari' kara para-upakāra*
> [*Caitanya-caritāmṛta, Ādi* 9.41]

Anyone who has taken birth in India should make his life perfect by becoming Kṛṣṇa conscious. Then he should distribute Kṛṣṇa consciousness all over the world.

Caitanya Mahāprabhu said one thing, that "Any Indian, any man who has taken birth on the soil of Bhāratavarṣa, India, he has got a special duty. And that duty is to spread Kṛṣṇa consciousness." Bhārata-bhūmite haila manuṣya-janma yāra, janma sārthaka kari kara para-upakāra. To do good to others, para-upakāra. So those Indians who are here, it is all right you are earning for some economic development, but at the same time, you try to make your life perfect by Kṛṣṇa consciousness and spread it to the foreigners as far as possible.

- ROOM CONVERSATION: JUNE 29, 1972

Prabhupāda: So, the Indians who are outside India, they have got a special duty. So far, our economic condition is concerned, as I explained yesterday, that one is destined to certain material comforts and discomforts, according to his body—already he has got. So, either you stay in India or you stay in America, the bodily comforts or sense gratification, that will be achieved either in India or America. What you are destined to achieve, you will have it because as soon as your body is manufactured, your standard of comfort and discomfort is also manufactured. In Bengal there is a proverb that yethā deoyā bhange, kapāla yābe saṅge(?): "Wherever you go, your fortune will go with you." Fortune and misfortune, that will also go with you. So Caitanya Mahāprabhu said one thing, that "Any Indian, any man who has taken birth on the soil of Bhāratavarṣa, India, he has got a special duty. And that duty is to spread Kṛṣṇa consciousness."

bhārata-bhūmite haila manuṣya-janma yāra
janma sārthaka kari' kara para-upakāra

To do good to others, para-upakāra. So those Indians who are here, it is all right you are earning for some economic development, but at the same time, you try to make your life perfect by Kṛṣṇa consciousness and spread it to the foreigners as far as possible. That's your duty, not that, that you are getting decent salary than India, and enjoy life and forget your culture. That is suicidal. You have got a culture... So, this culture is Vedic culture and Vedic culture means Kṛṣṇa conscious. As it is said in the Bhagavad-gītā, vedaiś ca sarvair aham eva vedyaḥ

(BG 15.15). Vedic culture means to understand Kṛṣṇa. One who has not understood Kṛṣṇa, he has no Vedic culture. But every Indian is supposed to have Vedic culture. And to have Vedic culture means to understand Kṛṣṇa. Therefore, all Indians, they should cultivate this Kṛṣṇa consciousness personally, make their life successful, and distribute it to the, our neighbors. Of course, I do not think... If you invite your neighbors, they do not come, you said?

Guest (1) (Indian man): Obviously, they have got some other work, this, that.

Prabhupāda: Hm. But anyway, because you are living in this country, you must have some friends. Whenever you talk with your friends, you talk about Kṛṣṇa. Don't waste your time in other ways. That will be beneficial for you and for your friends. And before talking about Kṛṣṇa, you should know about Kṛṣṇa. And you can know about Kṛṣṇa very easily by understanding Bhagavad-gītā. So read Bhagavad-gītā thoroughly. Try to understand it and you can distribute it. That is a great service to Kṛṣṇa, to your personal self, and to the person you are speaking about Kṛṣṇa. And four principles of impious life, as it is accepted by our Vedic followers, namely, no illicit sex, no meat-eating, no gambling, no intoxication. That will give you strength and over and above that, if you can chant Hare Kṛṣṇa mantra... You can chant. It is not difficult. There is no loss. You can chant. That will give you spiritual strength. And in this way try to become spiritually powerful and serve Kṛṣṇa. It doesn't matter where you are. It doesn't matter. Everywhere is Kṛṣṇa's kingdom. Sarva-loka-maheś-varam (BG 5.29). He is the proprietor everywhere. So, if you be in Kṛṣṇa consciousness, so wherever you may be, you'll be with Kṛṣṇa. And as soon as you remain with Kṛṣṇa, you are not living within this material world. You are living in the spiritual world. So, especially I request Indians, as it is ordered by Caitanya Mahāprabhu, that bhārata-bhūmite haila manuṣya-janma yāra: (CC Adi 9.41) "Anyone who has taken birth on the holy land of Bhāratavarṣa, India," janma sārthaka kari, "just make your life successful by Kṛṣṇa consciousness, and preach it." This is Caitanya Mahāprabhu's order. So, if you take it, you'll be happy, your neighbors will be happy, the world will be happy. And Kṛṣṇa-kathā means to present Kṛṣṇa as He is. Don't misinterpret by us..., just like some rascals do. Even a great scholar known all over the world practically in scholarly circle, he has practically vilified Kṛṣṇa by his so-called scholarship. Now he's suffering. He has lost himself; we have practically seen. So that is a great offense, to vilify saintly persons or God. That's great offense. So read Bhagavad-gītā as it is, present it as it is. Then your life is successful.

———

- University Lecture Calcutta, January 29, 1973

Prabhupāda: Śrī Gosvāmīpāda, Mr. Mohinath(?), Ladies and Gentlemen, I thank you very much for your kindly inviting me in this meeting to serve you to some extent according to my capacity. This Kṛṣṇa consciousness movement is not a new movement, started by me, but this movement was started by Kṛṣṇa Himself, five thousand years ago. I need not explain about this movement. Kṛṣṇa, in the Battlefield of Kurukṣetra, instructed Arjuna the Kṛṣṇa consciousness movement. The, in the Ninth Chapter it is said, *man-manā bhava mad-bhakto mad-yājī mām namaskuru* [Bg. 18.65]. This is Kṛṣṇa consciousness movement. "Always think of Kṛṣṇa," *man-manā. Bhava mad-bhakto*: "Just to become devotee of Kṛṣṇa." And *mām namaskuru*: "Offer obeisance's unto Me." Kṛṣṇa instructed, *mām eva ya prapadyante māyām etāṁ taranti te.* Kṛṣṇa instructed that He's the Supreme Personality. *Mattaḥ parataraṁ nānyat kiñcid asti dhanañjaya* [Bg. 7.7]. Kṛṣṇa instructed to surrender. *Sarva-dharmān parityajya mām ekaṁ śaraṇaṁ vraja* [Bg. 18.66]. So, this Kṛṣṇa consciousness movement is teaching this instruction of Kṛṣṇa. That's all. That is the order of Śrī Kṛṣṇa Caitanya Mahāprabhu. He is Kṛṣṇa Himself. *Kṛṣṇa-caitanya-nāmne.*

Śrī Rūpa Gosvāmī said:

> *namo mahā-vadānyāya*
> *kṛṣṇa-prema-pradāya te*
> *kṛṣṇāya kṛṣṇa-caitanya-*
> *nāmne gaura-tviṣe namaḥ*
> *[Cc. Madhya 19.53]*

When people understood Kṛṣṇa wrongly... Sometimes big scholars say "Sophistry," that "Kṛṣṇa wants full surrender." Others, they say, "Why you should fully surrender to Kṛṣṇa? We have got our own gods." Therefore Kṛṣṇa again came. As Gosvāmī Prabhupāda said: *rādhā kṛṣṇa-praṇaya vikṛtir, śrī caitanyākhyaṁ prakaṭam avyayam.* Rādhā and Kṛṣṇa, combined together, advented as Kṛṣṇa Caitanya Mahāprabhu to distribute *Kṛṣṇa-prema.* Because the mission of Lord Caitanya Mahāprabhu is to teach people how to develop love for Kṛṣṇa. As it is quoted by Gosvāmī Prabhupāda from *Śrīmad-Bhāgavatam*:

sa vai puṁsāṁ paro dharmo
yato bhaktir adhokṣaje
ahaituky apratihatā
yayātmā samprasīdati
[SB 1.2.6]

Actually, that is first-class religion. We do not say that Vedic religion is first-class or Christian religion is last-class. We do not say that. We say that religious system is first class which teaches the followers how to become lover of God. That is first-class religion. *Ahaituky apratihatā:* without any cause, and without being impeded. Caitanya Mahāprabhu's philosophy is like that, which is explained by Śrīla Viśvanātha Cakravartī Ṭhākura: *premā pumartho mahān ārādhyo bhagavān vrajeśa tanayas tad-dhāma vṛndāvanam.*

So, we are preaching this philosophy to the Western countries by the order of Śrī Caitanya Mahāprabhu. He desired,

pṛthivīte āche yata nagarādi grāma
sarvatra pracāra haibe more nāma

That is His prediction. It is nothing wonderful that we are doing. Simply we are trying to fulfill the prediction of Śrī Caitanya Mahāprabhu. But another order is there by Lord Caitanya Mahāprabhu that,

bhārata-bhūmite manuṣya janma haila yāra
janma sārthaka kari' karo paropakāra
[Cc. Ādi 9.41]

So that is lamentable. Now Śrī Caitanya Mahāprabhu's mission is being spread all over the world, but our Indian brothers are not joining it, although it is the order of Śrī Caitanya Mahāprabhu. *Bhārata-bhūmite manuṣya janma haila yāra.* He requested to the humankind who has taken birth in this land, in this *puṇya-bhūmi,* Bhāratavarṣa. Not to the cats and dogs, but to the human beings. That time has come now. If you want to prove that you are actually human being in this land, then you must take seriously the mission of Śrī Caitanya Mahāprabhu and spread all over the world. That is the order of Śrī Caitanya Mahāprabhu. And it is not very difficult. Caitanya Mahāprabhu says,

āmāra ājñāya guru hañā tāra sarva deśa
yāre dekha tāre kaha 'kṛṣṇa'-upadeśa
[Cc. Madhya 7.128]

To become guru, or spiritual master, is not very difficult task. Simply you have to follow the order of Śrī Caitanya Mahāprabhu, as he said. He accepted Kṛṣṇa: the Supreme Personality of Godhead. *Ārādhyo bhagavān vrajeśa tanayoḥ.* We have to simply preach that "You are searching after God, you great scientists, theologists, theosophists, mental speculators. You are searbhing after God, the Absolute Truth. Here is God, Kṛṣṇa." *Kṛṣṇas tu bhagavān svayam* [SB 1.3.28].

īśvaraḥ paramaḥ kṛṣṇaḥ
sac-cid-ānanda-vigrahaḥ
anādir ādir govindaḥ
sarva-kāraṇa-kāraṇam
[Bs. 5.1]

So, our task is very easy. Everything is there. Our Vedic literature is so full, so treasure of knowledge, great treasure of knowledge, we haven't got to make research, search out where is the truth. Truth is there and is explained in the *Śrīmad-Bhāgavatam: satyaṁ paraṁ dhīmahi* [SB 1.1.1]. Why don't you take it? The whole world is suffering for want of this knowledge. Before me, many swamis went in the Western countries, but they did not give the actual pure Vedic culture. They invented their own ways. Therefore, it was not very fruitive. It was not very satisfactory. People did not accept. Still there are so many yogis, the so-called yogis, are going there, exploiting the people, and coming back. But our Kṛṣṇa philosophy is taken very seriously in the Western countries. We have got now hundred and two branches all over the world. Only in America, we have got fifty branches. And other countries they have got fifty-two branches—in America, in Canada, in England, in France, in Germany, in Switzerland, in Japan, in Australia, in New Zealand. All over the world. So now we want some of the young men to come forward to become really *brāhmaṇas,* Vaiṣṇavas. Our Vedic culture is divided into four *varṇas: brāhmaṇa kṣatriya vaiśya śūdra.* Unfortunately, we are simply manufacturing *śūdras,* not *brāhmaṇas.* That is the defect of modern education. *Śūdra, śūdra* means *pari-caryātmakam kāryaṁ śūdra karma svabhāva-jam* [Bg. 18.44]. After education, every (indistinct) is hankering after a service.

That is *śūdra karma svabhāva-jam.* This is not perfect education. There must be *brāhmaṇas* who are independent. Cāṇakya Paṇḍita, whose name is still, still celebrated, he was prime minister of Mahārāja Candragupta, but he was not accepting a single paisa as salary. That was the, formerly, although there was monarchy, still there was a council of learned *brāhmaṇas* and sages. They used to advise the king. The *brāhmaṇas* did not take part in politics, but they gave advice, instruction to the kings, *rājarṣi. Imaṁ rājarṣayoḥ viduḥ.* The *rājarṣi* used to understand what is the values of life under the instruction of *brāhmaṇas,* and they execute the order of the *brāhmaṇas.* The people were happy. And because at the present moment such system is lost, people are confused and they are in frustration.

So, this Kṛṣṇa consciousness movement is all-embracing. It can solve all the problems of the world—political, social, economical, religious, everything. It is all-embracing. So, my request is that I am working now with my American disciples and European disciples. Why not Indians? I think in this meeting there are many young men, educated, learned scholars. Join this movement and, according to the order of Śrī Caitanya Mahāprabhu,

> *bhārata-bhūmite manuṣya janma haila yāra*
> *janma sārthaka kari' karo paropakāra*
> *[Cc. Ādi 9.41]*

This is the time to do welfare activities for the whole world. They are merged into confusion, everywhere. You know that in the Western countries, the hippy movements. What are the hippies? They're also educated, coming from very rich family also, but they do not like the way of envelopment as their fathers and grandfathers liked. They have rejected. So, this is the golden opportunity to preach the Kṛṣṇa cult all over the world. You are lamenting because a few yards of land have been taken away from your country as Pakistan, but if you spread this Kṛṣṇa consciousness movement, the whole world will become Hindustan. There is such potency; I give you my direct perception. People are hankering after it. So long I am in India, practically I am wasting my time. Outside India, this reception is taken so seriously that every part of my moment is properly utilized.

So, I have come to this university with a hope that some of you become really *brāhmaṇa*. The Sanskrit department is meant for *brāhmaṇas*. *Paṭhan pāṭhan yajana yājana dāna prati-graha*. A *brāhmaṇa* is called *paṇḍita*. Why? Because a *brāh-maṇa* must be learned. *Brāhmaṇa* is not called a fool. So, this department, Sanskrit department, is meant for the *brāhmaṇas*. So, I wish that some of you must join this movement, go to the foreign countries, preach this sublime cult of Caitanya Mahāprabhu. *Pṛthivīte āche yata nagarādi grāma*. There is great need. We have, of course, established so many temples, but still we require to establish temples, Rādhā-Kṛṣṇa temples, Caitanya Mahāprabhu's temple, in every village, every town of the world. Now from each and every of our centers, we are sending devotees in buses. They are going interior, into the villages of Europe and America, and they are very much well received. England especially, they are going village to village. They are very much well received. This cult is so nice. Even Christian priests, they are surprised. They are surprised. One of the priests in Boston, he issued pamphlet that "These boys, they're our boys, from Christian and Jews. Before this movement, they did not care to come to the churches even. Now they are mad after God." They are admitting. The Christian priestly class, they are not against us. Those who are saner class, they're admitting that "Swamijī's giving something tangible." Their fathers and forefathers come to me. They bow down. They say, "Swamijī, it is a great fortune for us that you have come to our country." So, I am alone working, and the movement is being appreciated. And if persons, scholars from this University come forward and teaches this movement, it is meant for that. *Brāhmaṇa's* business is that, preaching. *Brahmā jānāti*. One must know Brahman, and distribute the knowledge of *brahma-jñāna*. That is the business of *brāhmaṇas*.

So, I wanted to recite some stanzas from *Śrīmad-Bhāgavatam*, but there is no very much time. Long, long years ago, the father of Mahārāja Bhārata, under whose name this planet is called Bhāratavarṣa, so he instructed: *nāyaṁ deho deha-bhājāṁ nṛloke kaṣṭān kāmān arhati viḍ-bhujāṁ ye* [SB 5.5.1]. Here is the Fifth Canto of *Śrīmad-Bhāgavatam. Nāyaṁ deho deha-bhājāṁ nṛloke kaṣṭān kāmān arhati viḍ-bhujāṁ ye*. This human form of life, ayam deha... Ayam deha nṛloke: "in the human society." This is not meant for working very hard like the dogs and hogs. Kaṣṭān kāmān arhati *viḍ*-bhujāṁ ye. Simply by working hard, day and night, for sense gratification, this is done by the dogs and hogs. This is not meant for the human society. But, but at the present moment, people are being instructed in such a way... I've seen so many—especially in Calcutta—so many educated boys and girls, they are hankering after service. Day and night they are working. This is not the effect of education. The effect of education should be peaceful mind, peaceful living. That is the duty of the parents, of the guardians, of the government. When there is monarchical government... We see from the reign of Pṛthu Mahārāja. He was seeing that every *brāhmaṇa* is engaged in his occupational duty, every *kṣatriya* is employed, is engaged in occupational duty. Similarly, *vaiśya.* There was no question of unemployment. That is the first duty of the government to see. Neither there is division of the *brāhmaṇas, kṣatriyas, vaiśya, śūdra,* although it is made by Kṛṣṇa Himself: *cātur-varṇyaṁ mayā sṛṣṭaṁ guṇa-karma-vibhāgaśaḥ* [Bg. 4.13]. There have been so many anomalies in the society for want of this Vedic culture. Now here is the opportunity. People are accepting Kṛṣṇa consciousness movement very nicely. You can introduce this Vedic culture throughout the whole world. They're receiving.

So, the human form of life is especially meant for tapasya. *Tapo divyam.* Here it is said: *tapo divyaṁ putrakā yena sattvaṁ śuddhyed yasmād brahma-saukhyam anantam* [SB 5.5.1]. We are hankering after happiness, but happiness cannot be enjoyed so long our existence is not purified. So, for purifica-tion of our existence, we have to undergo *tapasya.* So, we are introducing this *tapasya* in nutshell. We are asking our students four principles, four regulative principles. No illicit sex life. Beyond marriage life, there is no sex. No intoxication, up to smoking and drinking tea. No meat-eating. No eggs, no fish. And no gambling. We are... And chanting this Hare Kṛṣṇa *mantra.* These five principles we are teaching. These four regulative principles, refraining from sinful activities.

These are the basic pillars of sinful activities: illicit sex, intoxication, meat-eating, and gambling. These are the four pillars of sinful life. That is... We get from the *śāstra*. Parīkṣit Mahārāja, he enunciated that Kali Yuga. He was... He ordered Kali Yuga, Kali, to live in these places. When he was ordered to go out of his kingdom, he said, "My dear Lord, everywhere is your kingdom. Where shall I live?" So he ordered him that "You live in these places, *striyaḥ sūnā pānaṁ dyūtaṁ yatra pāpaś caturvidhaḥ.*"

So, if we want to elevate the social condition, we shall teach people to become purified. Without being purified, simply so-called performance of religious system will not help. *Śrama eva hi kevalam* [SB 1.2.8]. *Svanuṣṭhitasya dharmasya saṁsiddhir hari-toṣaṇam* [SB 1.2.13]. We should teach people how to satisfy the Supreme Personality of Godhead. That is the injunction given by Sūta Gosvāmī in Naimiṣāraṇya, the assembly of great *brāhmaṇas*, learned *brāhmaṇas*.

> *ataḥ pumbhir dvija-śreṣṭhā*
> *varṇāśrama-vibhāgaśaḥ*
> *svanuṣṭhitasya dharmasya*
> *saṁsiddhir hari-toṣaṇam*
> *[SB 1.2.13]*

This is the philosophy. So, we are teaching this philosophy all over the world. They are being accepted. But I am doing it single-handed. But if some of you come and join us, it will be increased, and people will be very, very happy.

Thank you very much. Hare Kṛṣṇa. [break] That is my reply. Otherwise, I have not come to teach you something invented by me. I have come to teach you about Kṛṣṇa consciousness. And if you are not interested in Kṛṣṇa consciousness, then you must be amongst these four classes of men: *duṣkṛtinaḥ mūḍhāḥ, narādhama, māyayāpahṛta-jñānā.* This is my first reply. So far economic condition is concerned, then I may say, *eko yo bahūnāṁ vidadhāti kāmān.* God supplies you everything. God is supplying food to the elephant who is eating at a time forty kilos of food, and He's supplying to the ants also. So, your anxiety for food, that is not humanly. Even the cats and dogs, they are not anxious for their food. Even the birds, they rise early in the morning, they are also not anxious for the food. God has arranged for food, everyone. *Tal labhyate duḥkhavad anyataḥ sukham.* As you do not try for getting distress, it comes upon you according to your *karma,* similarly the so-called happiness also will come upon you without any endeavor. But because you have no faith in God, you are thinking that you will die out of hunger. That is not the position. *Tasyaiva hetoḥ prayateto kovido.* Our only business is how to become advanced in Kṛṣṇa consciousness. There is no other problem in human life. *Athāto brahma jijñāsā.* This is the human life. But you have been deviated from that high standard of life. You are now questioning in this way. That is my reply. Thank you very much.

———

- Room Conversation with Sanskrit Professor 8/13/1973-Paris

Professor: No, Bengali, no, I don't. But it doesn't matter.

Prabhupāda: Bhārata-bhūmite manuṣya-janma haila yāra (CC Adi 9.41). It is almost Sanskrit. "Anyone who has taken birth as human being in the land of Bhāratavarṣa," janma sārthaka kari, "making his life successful," kara para-upakāra. Para-upakāra. Para-upakāra means everyone is in slumber and considering himself that he is body, like cats and dogs. Therefore, they should be raised to the spiritual consciousness that "You are not cats and dogs. You are Brahman." Just realize "ahaṁ brahmāsmi." This is para-upakāra. So, we are doing that. We are awakening everyone. Uttiṣṭhataḥ jāgrataḥ prāpta-varaṁ nibodhata: "You have got now human being form of life. Now get up and make your life successful by spiritual realization." This is our message. Sarve sukhino bhavantu. By spiritual realization everyone will become happy. Without spiritual realization, nobody can become happy. This is our mission.

Professor: Thank you.

- Room Conversations, Vrndavana India, 9/11/1974

Prabhupāda: Then it will be andhā yathāndhair upanīyamānās (SB 7.5.31), one blind man is leading other blind men. What is that? They will all fall into ditch. Caitanya

Mahāprabhu therefore said, bharata-bhārata-bhūmite manuṣya-janma haila yāra (CC Adi 9.41), janma sārthaka kari': "First of all you be perfect, because you have got opportunity, and then do para-upakāra. Then go to other countries and deliver them." That is Caitanya Mahāprabhu. Not that you remain blind and go there. Just like all these rascal swamis and yogis, they are blind. They do not know what is spiritual life.

- Room Conversation, Atlanta GA, 3/2/1975

Prabhupāda: So not that Jagāi, Mādhāi five hundred years ago, now see at the present moment. They did not come to me after studying all the Vedas, and Vedantists. They come to me, I ask them that, "Don't commit these sinful activities and chant Hare Kṛṣṇa."That's all. Everyone can do, even the child can do. So, you are all educated men, you study this philosophy, try to understand, also join. It is your duty, because you are Indian. Caitanya Mahāprabhu entrusted this mission to the Indians.

bhārata-bhūmite haila manuṣya-janma yāra
janma sārthaka kari' kara para-upakāra
(CC Adi 9.41)

Indians are meant for doing good to others. That is Caitanya Mahāprabhu's mission. An Indian can become perfect because there is all the Vedic literature. Janma sārthaka kari'. First of all, you become perfect then preach the knowledge for other's benefit. This is Caitanya Mahāprabhu's. Now our leaders say, "Throw away these all śāstras in the water." This is going on. And what they have gained by throwing away? And actually, government is against us, against my movement in India. What can I do?

———

- Morning Walk 3/11/1975, London

Brahmānanda: Here you have to advertise to get six hundred.

Puṣṭa Kṛṣṇa: Or six.

Prabhupāda: And it was so nice to live there, spiritual atmosphere, on the bank of the Ganges and Yamunā. Immediately you go, you become spiritualized. Vṛndāvana is also like that. Therefore, Caitanya Mahāprabhu said, bhārata-bhūmite janma haila, manuṣya-janma haila. To get the human form of life born in India, that is a special prerogative. Bhārata-bhumite manuṣya-janma haila yāra (CC Adi 9.41). He is fifty percent-prepared by birth.

Brahmānanda: Just by birth.

Prabhupāda: Yes. And then, by culture, another fifty percent. But they have given up this culture. But the birthright fifty percent is already also there. Prayāga, severest cold, eh, I took bath in the Ganges. It is simply cutting. But still, they are taking bath and smearing over the body the ashes and sit down, chanting Hare Kṛṣṇa. No care "Wherefrom food will come? Where...?" No. That's in India still. (break) ...it is also like this, cloudy?

- Room Conversation with Indian Guest 3/13/1975, Tehran

Prabhupāda: It is my request that you are so many respectable Indian gentlemen here, and we are preaching Kṛṣṇa's message. You come forward. You learn more and join this mission. It is not meant for Mr. Attar; it is meant for everyone, especially for the Indians. Caitanya Mahāprabhu said that also, bhārata-bhūmite manuṣya-janma haila yāra (CC Adi 9.41). Bhārata-bhūmite means in the land of Bhāratavarṣa. Bhārata-bhūmi is considered puṇya-bhūmi. So, you are fortunate that you have taken birth as human being in India. It is the result of much pious activities. Indians are naturally Kṛṣṇa conscious. Now this gentleman, Mr. George, what is his name, full name?

Prabhupāda: Oh. The Canadian ambassador. He came to see me. He saw me in Delhi when our function was going on. He was speaking; he was so surprised. So, this movement has got good potency, and every one of you join.

bharata-bhūmite manuṣya-janma haila yāra
janma sārthaka kari 'kara para-upakāra
(CC Adi 9.41)

This is para-upakāra. The whole world is in darkness without Kṛṣṇa consciousness. So, enlighten them, para-upakāra. Human life is for para-upakāra; it is not animal life. To do good to others. Cats and dogs, they are selfish. But human life should be for para-upakāra. So, this is the biggest para-upakāra movement. And it is very easy to take part in it. You don't require to be very expert. You... Everything is there. You simply carry the message like peon.

———

- Morning Walk 6/13/1976, Detroit

Prabhupāda: This is fulfilling Caitanya Mahāprabhu's desire: pṛthivīte āche yata nagarādi-grāma. (CB Antya-khaṇḍa 4.126) Go to every village and town. So, you are doing very nice to satisfy the Lord. He wanted this. Pṛthivīte nagarādi—all over the world. So, when He meant all over the world, naturally He meant all the people of the world. Why Indian? Pṛthivīte āche yata nagarādi-grāma, it will include all the villages, towns, all over the world. That means all people of the world should take up this. Bhārata-bhūmite haila manuṣya-janma yāra (CC Adi 9.41). The Indians' duty is to carry the message, give it to the other people, and then they'll do. (break) ...a worldwide movement, not any particular. They may not misunderstand that this is Indian or Hindu. It is not that. Kṛṣṇa is meant for everyone. So, we shall have to go?

———

- Interview with Prof. O'Connel, Motilal and Shivaram 6/18/1976 Toronto

Prabhupāda: Oh, (laughs) Hare Kṛṣṇa. Motilal. (Converses in Hindi) That is Caitanya Mahāprabhu's mission, bhārata-bhūmite manuṣya-janma haila yāra janma sārthaka kari' kara para-upakāra (CC Adi 9.41). These things are unknown in the

Western countries. So, anyone who has taken birth in India, Bhārata-varṣa, they should make his..., one should make his life perfect by assimilating all these śāstras and preach the resultant action to the outsiders. That is Caitanya Mahāprabhu's mission-pṛthivīte āche yata nagarādi grāma. (CB Antya-khaṇḍa 4.126) So you Indians, you are here, you assimilate the teachings of Gītā, Bhāgavatam, Bhagavad-gītā, and Caitanya-caritāmṛta, and help these people. That is India's business.

- Room Conversation 6/24/1976 New Vrndavana

Prabhupāda: Therefore, Caitanya Mahāprabhu said to the Indians, that "You become perfect and go and give this knowledge to the rest of the world. They are all rascals." Bhārata-bhūmite haila manuṣya-janma yāra janma sārthaka kari' kara para-upakāra (CC Adi 9.41). It is para-upakāra, humanitarian. You may say "Why do you bother?" But as a human being, I bother. Every human being will do that. Kṛṣṇa comes, both-ering Himself. Yadā yadā hi dharmasya glānir bhavati bhārata (BG 4.7). "When these have become rascals, fools, I come, again advise them." So those who are servants of God, they are also doing the same thing, on behalf of God. Their position is therefore exalted.

- Evening Darshana 7/11/1976, New York

Prabhupāda: Therefore, we shall keep it dusty. If our heart is full of dust, cleanse it. That is intelligence. What is this, "My heart is dirty, let it be kept as dirty"? No, if it is dirty, cleanse it. It is the duty of every Indian to understand Kṛṣṇa and preach Kṛṣṇa consciousness movement to others. That is real Indian business. That is Caitanya Mahāprabhu's mission, that every one of you become Kṛṣṇa conscious and preach this Kṛṣṇa consciousness to others who are unaware of Kṛṣṇa. That is the injunction; that is Caitanya Mahāprabhu's mission. He said bhārata-bhūmite manuṣya-janma haila yāra (CC Adi 9.41). Anyone who has taken birth in India as a human being—not as dogs manuṣya, manuṣya means human—his duty is to become Kṛṣṇa conscious and preach to the other people for welfare activities. Bhārata-bhūmite manuṣya-janma haila yāra (CC Adi 9.41). We should mark this point, manuṣya-janma. He's not requesting the cats and dogs. So, in other words, that those who are not taking, Indians... Bhagavad-gītā is known to everyone, every Indian knows. But if he does not preach this Kṛṣṇa consciousness, then he is not to be counted as human being. Because He says manuṣya-janma haila yāra. If we claim to be human being, born in India, it is our duty to understand the value of life from Bhagavad-gītā and preach this cult to others to do real welfare activities.

Prabhupāda: Sthito 'smi gata-sandehaḥ. "Now all my doubts are over. Now I shall kill." Why did you not say this to your European audience?

Indian man (3): Because I don't know the Gītā myself that good.

Prabhupāda: Then why do you preach? First of all, know, then preach. If you did not know, you should not preach. Therefore, Caitanya Mahāprabhu said, janma sārthaka kari' kara para-upakāra (CC Adi 9.41). First of all, make your life perfect, then try to make others perfect. Don't cheat others. So, when Arjuna actually became intelligent, he said sthito 'smi gata-sandehaḥ kariṣye vacanaṁ tava. This is understanding. "Yes, now I am situated in my proper understanding, I shall carry out Your order."

- Room Conversation 8/2/1976 New Mayapur (French-Farm)

Prabhupāda: Recognition means you become the dearest servant of Kṛṣṇa. Then what do you want more? If Kṛṣṇa recognizes that "You are My most dear servant," then what do you want more? Yāre dekha tāre kaha 'kṛṣṇa'-upadeśa (CC Madhya 7.128). So, this message was to be carried by all Indians. That is Caitanya Mahāprabhu's desire.

bhārata-bhūmite haila manuṣya-janma yāra
janma sārthaka kari' kara para-upakāra
(CC Adi 9.41)

This is para-upakāra. So, all Indians should take up this mission and do welfare activity. That is India's special function.

- Evening Darshan 8/10/1976, Tehran

Prabhupāda: Therefore, Caitanya Mahāprabhu's mission is that anyone who has taken birth in India, make his life successful, and then preach this knowledge to the outside world. The exact word,

bhārata bhūmite manuṣya janma haila yāra
janma sārthaka kari 'kara para-upakāra
(CC Adi 9.41)

Outside India they are in darkness. So, it is the duty of the Indian to make his life perfect and spread his spiritual knowledge to the outside world. That is real welfare activity in the human society. That we are trying to do. Unfortunately, they have not taken very seriously what glorious activities for India we are doing. They do not understand.

———

- Room Conversation 8/14/1976, Mumbai

Prabhupāda: No, you come and preach. The country is going to hell, the human society is going to hell for misguidance. These rascal leaders, they're going to hell themselves and they're leading others. Andhā yathāndhair upanīyamānās te 'pīśa-tantryām uru-dāmni baddhāḥ (SB 7.5.31). These fools and rascals are leading, they are going to hell, and they are taking the followers to the hell. This is going on. Stop this. At least in India. Save. That is real para-upakāra. That is Caitanya Mahāprabhu's mission.

bhārata-bhūmite haila manuṣya-janma yāra
janma sārthaka kari' kara para-upakāra
(CC Adi 9.41)

Para-upakāra. Our India is not meant for exploiting others. Doing good to others, that is India's mission. Our teachers, our ācāryas, do not teach us "Go and exploit others and bring money"—British Empire. This is not India.

Prabhupāda: This is Indian culture. Even the enemy comes, "Yes, please come, you stay." But later on, they took advantage: "Oh, they are very liberal, enter there." And still, we are liberal. "Please come here, stay here and take prasādam free, and chant Hare Kṛṣṇa." Open to everyone. I shall manage anyway, I shall travel, still I shall lay down my life and bring money. Come here, stay. Still, we are liberal.

This is Caitanya Mahāprabhu's mission, janma sārthaka kari' kara para-upakāra (CC Adi 9.41). First of all, make your life successful by Kṛṣṇa consciousness. Then do good to others. Yesterday, I think, in Tehran, one boy came. He proposed that is it not good to help others? I immediately challenged, "What you have got you can help? What is your asset?" You cannot help.

It is simply bogus proposition. If you can help, you can simply help by spreading Kṛṣṇa consciousness, as Caitanya Mahāprabhu said, yāre dekha tāre kaha kṛṣṇa-upadeśa (CC Madhya 7.128). "Sir, I have come to you." "Why?" "To request you that you become Kṛṣṇa conscious." "How?" Man-manā bhava mad-bhaktaḥ, "Always think of Me, just become My devotee, offer little obeisances." Anyone can do, a child can do.

———

- Morning Walk 8/23/1976, Hyderabad

Prabhupāda: The modern civilization is deluxe edition of animal life. That's all. Animal-deluxe edition. That's all. They do not know what is the aim of life. So, as you are life member, you should study our, this philosophy. Life members, they are given books. And preach this, and save this human... That is the duty. Paropakāra. Human life is meant for paropakāra. That is Caitanya Mahāprabhu's mission.

bhārata-bhūmite haila manuṣya-janma yāra
janma sārthaka kari' kara para-upakāra
(CC Adi 9.41)

Because they are in darkness, all rascals, mūḍha. Nābhijānāti. They do not know anything. And they're puffed up by their false education, false knowledge. Ahaṅkāra-vimūḍhātmā. "Huh! I have no engagement." Vimūḍhātmā. Kartāham iti manyate. They do not know how nature's law is working. Do they not know?

———

- Room Conversation with Mr. Tombe (M.L.A.) 12/25/1976, Mumbai

Prabhupāda: So, what kind of leading? He's imperfect. So, he cannot lead. Then there will be some mistake and chaos. Just like Caitanya Mahāprabhu said... He said bhārata-bhūmite manuṣya-janma haila yāra (CC Adi 9.41). You understand little Bengali?

bhārata-bhūmite haila manuṣya-janma yāra
janma sārthaka kari' kara para-upakāra
(CC Adi 9.41)

So, Indians, they can make their life perfect by following this Vedic literature, and they can lead the whole world. This is Caitanya Mahāprabhu's. First of all, you become perfect by taking lessons from the Vedic literature.

———

- Morning Walk and Room Conversation - - December 26, 1976, Bombay

Prabhupāda: If you speak the truth, then you take the quotation of Kṛṣṇa. Now every Indian should take part in this great movement. Every Indian. That is the Caitanya Mahāprabhu's order.

bhārata-bhūmite haila manuṣya-janma yāra
janma sārthaka kari' kara para-upakāra

Prabhupāda: Then how shall I conduct my business? A big, big establishment. This is another problem. But Kṛṣṇa is doing His own business. But practically seeing. This is India's business. Bhārata-bhūmite manuṣya-janma haila yāra (CC Adi 9.41). Manuṣya-janma, not the cats and dogs, but those who have taken the human form. It is their business. Caitanya Mahāprabhu says, bhārata-bhūmite manuṣya-janma haila yāra (CC Adi 9.41), janma sārthaka-First of all, make your life successful by understanding the philosophy. Then, janma sārthaka kari' kara para-upakāra, preach this philosophy all over the world. That is para-upakāra. So actually, that is being done. They understand, they are understanding this philosophy. There is struggle now in foreign countries. There is opposition now. Who will explain what is the opposition?

———

- ROOM CONVERSATION -- DECEMBER 26, 1976, BOMBAY

Prabhupāda: Oh yes, you are welcome always. Whenever you find time. (Hindi) Janma sārthaka kari' kara para-upakāra (CC Adi 9.41). This is Caitanya. First of all, make your life successful. That successful means yei kṛṣṇa-tattva-vettā sei guru haya (CC Madhya 8.128), to understand Kṛṣṇa thoroughly. Then you become guru. When you understand Kṛṣṇa, then you are janma sārthaka. And then you can speak para-upakāra. Otherwise, it is not possible. Without Kṛṣṇa tattva-jñāna, if we become leader, that will not take... yei kṛṣṇa-tattva-vettā sei guru haya (CC Madhya 8.128). What is that?

kibā vipra, kibā nyāsī, śūdra kene naya
yei kṛṣṇa-tattva-vettā, sei 'guru' haya

Translation

"Whether one is a brāhmaṇa, a sannyāsī or a śūdra — regardless of what he is — he can become a spiritual master if he knows the science of Kṛṣṇa."

- Press Interview -- December 31, 1976, Bombay

Prabhupāda: Most important movement. (Hindi) You are in a good position. Try to convince others. Life should be for para-upakāra. Not exploiting. This is India's mission. That is Caitanya Mahāprabhu says,

bhārata-bhūmite haila manuṣya-janma yāra
janma sārthaka kari' kara para-upakāra
(CC Ādi 9.41)

This is India's... Anyone who has taken birth in India, first of all make his life perfect by understanding the śāstra. The gist of śāstra is Bhagavad-gītā. And then distribute the knowledge. Para-upakāra. This should be India's mission. India hasn't got to learn from anywhere else. Everything is there. Let him understand the whole philosophy of life perfectly and distribute this. This is India's mission. So, I have tried alone on this point. So, I have got little success. And before me so many swamis, yogis went there. They came and go. No effect. Now I have created a community which will continue. They're now saying, "American Hindus." Therefore, there is opposition. They understand, "Now it will stand." It is not that Vivekananda's daridra-nārāyaṇa-sevā.

- - -

- Evening Conversation -- January 25, 1977, Puri

Prabhupāda: That is another thing. But these three words, that "Kṛṣṇa is the Supreme Lord; you are servant; and chant Hare Kṛṣṇa"—bas, preaching complete. Very simple thing and the sublime instruction. Everyone can become guru by simply teaching these three words. Not sophisticated, but he must also understand not blindly. Bhārata-bhūmite haila manuṣya-janma yāra, janma sārthaka kari (CC Adi 9.41)'. He must also understand these three words perfectly. Then wherever he speaks, he'll be successful. Not that "For you I am speaking. I can do everything independently." No. I am also servant of Kṛṣṇa. Realized. This is realization.

- - -

- Room Conversation -- February 3, 1977, Bhuvanesvara

Prabhupāda: Here is opportunity for his getting out of the clutches of māyā, daivī hy eṣā guṇamayī mama māyā (BG 7.14), and they are being misled, the so-called science and nasty philosophy and economics and making them, training them as demons and rākṣasas. What is this civilization? So, our movement is against this demonic civilization. It is really para-upakāra.

> *bhārata-bhūmite haila manuṣya-janma yāra*
> *janma sārthaka kari' kara para-upakāra*
> *(CC Adi 9.41)*

And this is India's mission, Caitanya Mahāprabhu's mission, para-upakāra. So... And Kṛṣṇa also confirms, ya idaṁ paramaṁ guhyaṁ mad-bhakteṣv abhidhāsyati, na ca tasmād... (Bg 18.68). You'll be recognized by Kṛṣṇa. Simply go on sincerely working for this movement. Nobody can defeat you.

———

- Room Conversation -- February 14, 1977, Mayapura

Prabhupāda: Anyone who has understood the value of Hare Kṛṣṇa, he is saved. But we should not simply keep ourselves saved. We should think for others. That is para-upakāra. And that you cannot do unless you are in the safe position. Janma sārthaka kari'. If you become polluted, then you cannot do. That is the secret. If you are not polluted, then you can do. Otherwise, it will be show only, no effect. This is the secret. Janma sārthaka kari' kara para-upakāra (CC Adi 9.41). So, things are very easy, not at all difficult. If you follow, then you can do good to others.

. . .

Prabhupāda: Then finished. In order to check others, if we become carried away, (laughing) then finish all business. To save them from being washed away by māyā, if we become washed away, then where is the hope? Therefore, Caitanya Mahāprabhu said, janma sārthaka kari' kara para-upakāra (CC Adi 9.41). Be strong so that you may not be rascal, and then you can do; others you can check. Otherwise, it will be impossible. How it is possible? A man is drowning.

- Room Conversation -- March 22, 1977, Bombay

Prabhupāda: You have to accept another body. Then you go on. Why this human form of life should be lost in this way? So at least to try to give this knowledge to the people in general is para-upakāra. This is para-upakāra. And that is Caitanya Mahāprabhu's gift. India can especially do it.

bharata-bhūmite haila manuṣya-janma yāra
janma sārthaka kari' kara para-upakāra
(CC Adi 9.41)

(Hindi) (break) ...these and some great man, not that they think bad. And if somebody checks me, how great enemy he is.

Tamāla Kṛṣṇa: The natural tendency of the people here is to be God conscious, but the government is artificially checking. Whether this new government will be any different?

- Room Conversation with Ratan Singh Rajda (Member of Parliament) -- March 27, 1977, Bombay

Prabhupāda: Unless you come to that knowledge, there is no question of welfare activities. That knowledge is available in India. India should understand. That is Caitanya Mahāprabhu's mission. Bhārata-bhūmite manuṣya janma haila yāra (CC Adi 9.41). Not only India, but he must be a human being. Not only human being, but also systematic human society. (break) Of course, we are trying to give this knowledge. These American, Europeans, they are taking it. It should be done very systematically, not alone tried.

- Interview with Mr. Koshi (Asst. Editor of The Current Weekly) -- April 5, 1977, Bombay

Prabhupāda: That is not possible. Similarly, how many men will understand or not understand, that is not the consideration. But we have got in India such exalted knowledge. We must cultivate and distribute knowledge as far as possible. It is our duty. That is Caitanya Mahāprabhu's mission. Bhārata-bhūmite manuṣya-janma haila yāra (CC Adi 9.41). You understand Bengali?

Mr. Koshi: No.

Prabhupāda: "Anyone who has taken birth as human being in India, janma sārthaka kari' kara para-upakāra, first of all make your life successful by understanding what is life, and then distribute." This is Caitanya Mahāprabhu. You have got this asset. You have rejected.

———

- Morning Talk -- April 5, 1977, Bombay

Prabhupāda: Para-duḥkha-duḥkhī, kṛpāmbudhi. My Guru Mahārāja used to say prāṇa āche yāṅra se'retu(?) pracāra. One who is living being, he can preach. Dead body cannot. One who is actually a living being, he can preach. And Caitanya Mahāprabhu said bhārata-bhūmite haila manuṣya-janma yāra (CC Adi 9.41). One who is a man, he will be interested in this. Cats and dogs, it is not possible. Bhārata-bhūmite haila kukkura-janma yāra, eka... Manuṣya. To give knowledge of Bhagavad-gītā, this is India's prerogative. And India can distribute this knowledge. And the government has to consent. And they are misinterpreting this. I wanted to fight them, but...

———

- Room Conversation with Ratan Singh Rajda M.P. 'Nationalism and Cheating' -- April 15, 1977, Bombay

Prabhupāda: So, He declares that bhārata-bhūmite manuṣya-janma haila yāra: (CC Adi 9.41) "Anyone who has taken birth as human being, not cats and dogs..." Cats and dogs, they simply jump whole night: "Gow! Gow! Gow!" That is another... We find so many dogs, whole night busy, watching. Whose property he is watching? But he... He has got this business, very busy. As soon as some motorcycle or some..., "Gow! Gow! Gow! Gow! Gow! Gow!" watching, watching, watching. So therefore, this is business of cats and dogs. But human being's business is different. Therefore Caitanya Mahāprabhu said, bhārata-bhūmite haila manuṣya-janma yāra: (CC Adi 9.41) "Anyone who has taken birth as a human being in India, bhārata-bhūmi..." Janma sārthaka kari' kara para-upakāra: "First of all make your life perfect"—you have got the opportunity, Vedic culture—"and then distribute the knowledge all over the world for doing good to the whole human society." That will glorify the prestige of India. So why not continue this? Let there be an institution fully following the principles of Bhagavad-gītā, Bhagavad-gītā As It Is.

- Room Conversation with Ram Jethmalani (Parliament Member) -- April 16, 1977, Bombay:

Ram Jethmalani: Our own intellect tells us that our intellect is finite. There are certain things which you can't reason, and that also I grant that you are right. One has to see these things with one's secret eye.

Prabhupāda: (Hindi) This is the right of Bhāratavarṣa. Of this Caitanya Mahāprabhu says,

bhārata-bhūmite haila manuṣya-janma yāra
janma sārthaka kari' kara para-upakāra
(CC Adi 9.41)

Ei para-upakāra, to distribute this knowledge to the whole human society. The human (Hindi). This is the real human service, to give them knowledge.

Girirāja: I know you haven't eaten all day.

Prabhupāda: (Hindi conversation)

Ram Jethmalani: What is your normal dinnertime?

———

- Room Conversation Meeting with Dr. Sharma (from Russia) -- April 17, 1977, Bombay

Prabhupāda: It is not to be accepted blindly. (break) So you are in Russia, educated young man. You can do something. Everyone can do something.

bharata-bhūmite haila manuṣya-janma yāra
janma sārthaka kari' kara para-upakāra
(CC Adi 9.41)

Bhārata-bhūmi, anyone who has taken birth in Bhārata-bhūmi, especially in high family, it is the duty of every Indian to understand this sublime knowledge and distribute it to the world. Para-upakāra. That is Caitanya Mahāprabhu's mission. Because we have got this knowledge, everything. This knowledge you cannot have anywhere.

———

- Second Meeting with Mr. Dwivedi -- April 24, 1977, Bombay

Prabhupāda: He is... Īśvaraḥ paramaḥ kṛṣṇaḥ sac-cid-ānanda-vigrahaḥ (Bs. 5.1), anādir ādir... Anādi. (Hindi) You have got so exalted knowledge in India. You have kept it packed. And you are going to beg from others? Take this knowledge of Bhagavad-gītā and assimilate it, make your life successful, and distribute it throughout the whole world. That I want. (Hindi) Knowledge, real knowledge, is in India. (Hindi) Therefore Caitanya Mahāprabhu said,

bhārata-bhūmite haila manuṣya-janma yāra
janma sārthaka kari' kara para-upakāra
(CC Adi 9.41)

Indians, they are fortunate. They have got their birth in Bhāratavarṣa. The knowledge is here. So, assimilate this knowledge. Make your life successful and distribute it to persons outside India. That is paropakāra. That is real paropakāra. That is real sevā. But sevā, no. It is dayā. The sevā cannot be used. Sevā means offered to the superior. And to the inferior, if you want to do something, that is dayā.

———

- Evening Darsana -- May 12, 1977, Hrishikesh

Prabhupāda: (Hindi) It will distribute India's glories. People will feel obliged to India, that "We have got this knowledge from India." Actually, knowledge is here. There is no such knowledge all over the world.

bharata-bhūmite haila manuṣya-janma yāra
janma sārthaka kari' kara para-upakāra
(CC Adi 9.41)

Paropakāra. India is meant for paropakāra. India is not meant for exploiting others. But unfortunately, the knowledge is... Sarasvatī jñāna-khale yathā satī. We have got the store of knowledge, but we have kept it locked up, not distributed to the world. They are called jñāna-khala. One who has knowledge but he does not want to distribute it, that is, they are termed as jñāna-khala. So, we should not be jñāna-khala.

————

- Room Conversation with Sri Narayana and Rama-Krsna Bajaj -- October 31, 1977, Vrndavana

Prabhupāda: That is Bhagavān, Kṛṣṇa. Ye yathā māṁ prapadyate (Hindi) Para-upakāra. This is the mission of Caitanya Mahāprabhu, para-upakāra. Especially those who have taken birth in India...

bharata-bhūmite haila manuṣya-janma yāra
janma sārthaka kari' kara para-upakāra
(CC Adi 9.41)(Hindi)

This is Indian culture, para-upakāra. Indian culture is not meant for exploiting others. Para-upakāra. That is human life, para-upakāra. And that is Caitanya Mahāprabhu's mission. Bhārata, especially...

As I mentioned in the introduction, having only scratched the surface from what Srila Prabhupada taught on the subject of taken birth as human beings in Bharat-varsha and or this planet (Earth).

-An Address given in Bombay late 1960s

Śrīla Prabhupāda said: "Gentlemen, do not for a moment think that my Gurudeva wants to put a complete brake on the modern civilization—an impossible feat. But let us learn from him the art of making the best use of a bad bargain, and let us understand the importance of this human life, which is fit for the highest development of true consciousness. The best use of this rare human life should not be neglected. As it is said in the Śrīmad-Bhāgavatam (11.9.29):

> *labdhva sudurlabham idam bahu-sambhavante*
> *manusyam arthadam anityam apiha dhirah*
> *turnam yateta na pated anu mrtyu yavan*
> *nihsreyasaya visayah khalu sarvatah syat*

"This human form of life is obtained after many, many births, and although it is not permanent, it can offer the highest benefits. Therefore, a sober and intelligent man should immediately try to fulfil his mission and attain the highest profit in life before another death occurs. He should avoid sense gratification, which is available in all circumstances."

Closing Statement

There are two scenarios that comes to mind to be considered *Fortunate or Unfortunate* In the "Bhagavad-Gita As It Is" Lord Sri Krishna instructed Arjuna His principle student in the 18th Chapter text 63 iti *te jnanam akhyatam guhyad guyataram maya vimrsyaitad asesena yathecchasi tatha kuru.*

Thus, I have explained to you the most confidential of all knowledge Deliberate on this fully and then do what you wish to do.

In other words, the Lord never interferes with your choice but once that is done destiny takes its course.

The beauty of the truth is that it never changes, it has nothing to do with what you, myself or anyone thinks or believes we just have the option to accept or not accept. It will never change.

Water is always wet. So, if one take advantage of these timeless instructions given by Lord Chaitanya through the medium of Srila Prabhupada's teachings instantly becomes *fortunate.*

All those people who on this planet, as well as Bharata-varsha (India) where there are so many spiritual opportunities, hopefully will take advantage of this facility easily.

To not plunge down into the category of the *unfortunate*, that is, after hearing all these instructions, will do what is necessary for themselves and the world.

I will do my part and continue to pray for the welfare of everyone. Hare Krishna! Jaya Srila Prabhupada!

Shambhu dasa

About the Compiler

Shambhu Das (Kenneth Pickett), born in Stuttgart Germany, 1958, is the son of a career military soldier and the middle child of seven (five boys and two girls). In the summer of 1973 in the famous childhood neighborhood "Riggs-Park" Washington D.C. after just turning fifteen, and under the tutelage of Sriman Balaka das Prabhu, Shambhu decided to become an inspiring disciple and proved to be a renowned foot soldier in the army of His Divine Grace A.C. Bhaktivedanta Swami Maharaja Srila Prabhupada's "Sankirtan" preaching mission.

Having traveled extensively throughout the world, especially India, preaching and distributing His Divine Grace's transcendental literature, Shambhu also sings and mastered many traditional, conventional musical instruments.

Note: In the First-page-photo

Srila Prabhupada seats on the Vysasana in Broolyn N.Y. Famous Sri Radha-Govinda Temple Henry Street in 1973 a young "Shambhu" prabhu standing.

Verses and Other References

Sri Isopanishad Text-3

Bhagavad-Gita As It Is Chapter-6-txt-41-43

Srimad Bhagavatam Canto-4-Chapter-23-txt-28

The Journey of Self Discovery "Conversation Dr.Benford"

Srimad Bhagavatam Canto-7-Chapter-6-txt

1,2,14,15

Srimad Bhagavatam Canto-6-Chapter-16-txt-41

Science of Self-Realization pg-105

Jaiva-Dharma-Chapter-16

Introduction of Bhagavad-Gita As It Is "Sanatana-Dharma"

Srimad Bhagavatam 5th Canto-Chapter-19-Text

19, 21, 22, 23, 24, 25, 28

Srimad Bhagavatam Canto-6-Chapter-16-txt-58

Mumbia-Lecture-Address-Mumbia-late-1960's

Chaitanya-Charitamrta-Madhya-lila-Chapter-25-txt-264

Conversation: Lt. David Mozee Chicago Police Dept. July-1975

Room Conversation: June 29, 1972

Lecture: University Calcutta, January 29, 1973

Room Conversation: Sanskrit Professor Paris 8/13/2973

Room Conversation: Vrndavana India 9/11/1974

Room Conversation: Atlanta GA 3/2/1975

Morning Walk: London England 3/11/1975

Room Conversation: Indian Guest Tehran Iran 3/13/1975

Morning Walk Detroit Michigan 6/13/1976

Conversation Interview Toronto Canada 6/18/1976

Room Conversation: Vrndavana India 6/24/1976

Evening Darshan: New York, Manhattan 7/11/1976

Room Conversation: New Mayapur (French-Farm) 8/2/1976

Evening Darshan: Tehran Iran 8/10/1976

Room Conversation: Mumbai India 8/14/1976

Morning Walk, Hyderabad, India 8/23/1976

Room Conversation: Mr. Tombe (M.L.A.) Mumbai India 12/25/1976

Morning Walk Conversation: Bombay India 12/26/1976

Room Conversation -- December 26, 1976, Bombay

Press Interview: Mumbai India 12/31/1976

Evening Conversation: Jagannatha Puri 1/25/1977

Room Conversation -- February 3, 1977, Bhuvanesvara

Room Conversation: Sridham Mayapura India 2/14/1977

Room Conversation: Bombay India 3/22/1977

Room Conversation: Ratan Singh Rajda (Member of Parliament) Bombay India 3/27/1977

Interview: Mr. Koshi (Asst. Editor the Current Weekly) Bombay India 4/5/1977

Morning Talk Conversation: Bombay India 4/5/1977

Room Conversation with Ratan Singh Rajda M.P. 'Nationalism and Cheating' --April 15, 1977, Bombay

Room Conversation: Ram Jethumalani (Parliament-Member) Bombay India 4/16/1977

Room Conversation: Dr. Sharma (From Russia) Bombay India 4/17/1977

Conversation-Meeting: Mr. Dwivedi Bombay India 4/24/1977

Evening Darshan: Hrishikesh India 5/12/1977

Room Conversation: Sri Narayana and Rama Krsna Baja Vrndavan India 10/31/1977